Better Homes and Gardens®

Fast-Fixin' Chicken

Our seal assures you that every recipe in *Fast-Fixin' Chicken*
has been tested in the Better Homes and Gardens® Test Kitchen.
This means that each recipe is practical and reliable,
and meets our high standards of taste appeal.

BETTER HOMES AND GARDENS® BOOKS
Editor: Gerald M. Knox
Art Director: Ernest Shelton
Managing Editor: David A. Kirchner
Copy and Production Editors: James D. Blume, Marsha Jahns,
    Rosanne Weber Mattson, Mary Helen Schiltz

Food and Nutrition Editor: Nancy Byal
Department Head, Cook Books: Sharyl Heiken
Associate Department Heads: Sandra Granseth,
    Rosemary C. Hutchinson, Elizabeth Woolever
Senior Food Editors: Julia Malloy, Marcia Stanley,
    Joyce Trollope
Associate Food Editors: Linda Henry, Mary Major,
    Diana McMillen, Mary Jo Plutt, Maureen Powers,
    Martha Schiel, Linda Foley Woodrum
Recipe Development Editor: Marion Viall
Test Kitchen Director: Sharon Stilwell
Test Kitchen Photo Studio Director: Janet Pittman
Test Kitchen Home Economists: Lynn Blanchard,
    Jean Brekke, Kay Cargill, Marilyn Cornelius,
    Jennifer Darling, Maryellyn Krantz, Lynelle Munn,
    Dianna Nolin, Marge Steenson

Associate Art Directors: Linda Ford Vermie, Neoma Alt West,
    Randall Yontz
Assistant Art Directors: Lynda Haupert, Harijs Priekulis,
    Tom Wegner
Senior Graphic Designers: Jack Murphy, Stan Sams,
    Darla Whipple-Frain
Graphic Designers: Mike Burns, Sally Cooper, Blake Welch,
    Brian Wignall, Kimberly Zarley

Vice President, Editorial Director: Doris Eby
Executive Director, Editorial Services: Duane L. Gregg

President, Book Group: Fred Stines
Director of Publishing: Robert B. Nelson
Vice President, Retail Marketing: Jamie Martin
Vice President, Direct Marketing: Arthur Heydendael

FAST-FIXIN' CHICKEN
Editor: Martha Schiel
Copy and Production Editor: Marsha Jahns
Graphic Designer: Sally Cooper
Electronic Text Processor: Donna Russell
Contributing Photographer: Mike Dieter
Food Stylists: Dianna Nolin, Janet Pittman

On the cover: Honey of a Chicken (see recipe, page 46)

Contents

Special Delivery

With *Fast-Fixin' Chicken*, neither stress, nor job, nor lack of time will ever again keep you from your appointed mealtimes. We've put together a first-class package of ready-when-you-are chicken and turkey entrées, postmarked for your table. All are delivered in 45 minutes or less—many in as little as 30 minutes—so that you can give your family the special handling they deserve.

25 minutes
Raspberry-Rosé Turkey Steaks
(see recipe, page 9)

30 minutes
Orange-Papaya Chicken
(see recipe, page 30)

20 minutes
Turkey-Veggie Pitas
(see recipe, page 71)

Mustard-Herb Chicken

Total time: 40 minutes

¼ cup butter *or* margarine
1 tablespoon Dijon-style mustard
1 teaspoon lemon pepper
1 teaspoon dried oregano, crushed
¼ teaspoon crushed red pepper

● Preheat the broiler. Meanwhile, for the mustard glaze, in a small saucepan combine butter or margarine, mustard, lemon pepper, oregano, and crushed red pepper. Cook and stir till butter or margarine is melted.

Brushing on the mustard glaze just before turning the chicken and during the last 5 minutes of broiling keeps the herbs in it from burning.

2 to 2½ pounds meaty chicken pieces (breasts, wings, thighs, and drumsticks)

● Place chicken pieces, skin side down, on an unheated rack in a broiler pan. Broil 4 to 5 inches from the heat for 15 to 18 minutes or till lightly browned. Brush chicken with mustard glaze. Turn pieces and broil about 15 minutes more or till meat is no longer pink. Brush with mustard glaze and broil for 5 minutes more. Makes 4 servings.

Grilling directions: Prepare as above, *except* grill chicken pieces, skin side down, on an uncovered grill directly over *medium* coals for 20 minutes. Brush with mustard glaze. Turn and grill for 10 to 20 minutes more or till done, brushing with glaze during the last 5 minutes.

This fleet-footed fowl is no dumb cluck. Follow this many-flavored fella and he'll lead you to the recipes in this book that you can prepare in 25 minutes or less.

Lime-Pepper Chicken

½ teaspoon finely shredded
   lime peel
⅓ cup lime juice
2 tablespoons cooking oil
1 teaspoon dried thyme,
   crushed
1 teaspoon cracked black
   pepper
½ teaspoon garlic salt

● Preheat the broiler. Meanwhile, for sauce, in a small mixing bowl stir together lime peel, lime juice, cooking oil, thyme, pepper, and garlic salt. Set mixture aside.

To grill, prepare the recipe as directed, *except* grill the chicken pieces, skin side down, on an uncovered grill, directly over *medium* coals for 20 minutes, brushing occasionally with sauce. Turn and grill for 10 to 20 minutes more or till done, brushing often with sauce.

2 to 2½ pounds meaty
   chicken pieces (breasts,
   wings, thighs, and
   drumsticks)

● Place chicken, skin side down, on an unheated rack in a broiler pan. Brush with sauce. Broil 4 to 5 inches from the heat for 15 to 18 minutes or till lightly browned, brushing often with sauce. Turn chicken. Brush with sauce. Broil for 10 to 15 minutes more or till no longer pink, brushing often with sauce. Serves 4.

Chutney Chicken

Total time: 35 minutes

2 to 2½ pounds meaty chicken pieces (breasts, wings, thighs, and drumsticks)	● Preheat the broiler. Place chicken pieces, skin side down, on an unheated rack in a broiler pan. Broil 4 to 5 inches from the heat for 15 to 18 minutes or till chicken is lightly browned.
½ of a 9-ounce jar chutney **1 tablespoon butter *or* margarine** **1 tablespoon lemon juice** **⅛ teaspoon pepper**	● Meanwhile, for chutney sauce, in a small saucepan stir together chutney, butter or margarine, lemon juice, and pepper. Cook mixture over medium heat till butter melts and mixture bubbles, stirring occasionally.
Green onion fans (optional)	● Turn chicken pieces and broil for 10 to 15 minutes more or till no longer pink, brushing chicken with some of the chutney sauce during the last 2 minutes of broiling. Spoon remaining chutney sauce over chicken. Garnish with green onion fans, if desired (see photo, below). Makes 4 servings.

Grilling directions: Prepare as above, *except* grill chicken pieces, skin side down, on an uncovered grill directly over *medium* coals for 20 minutes or till lightly browned. Turn pieces. Grill for 10 to 20 minutes more or till chicken is done, brushing with some of the sauce during the last 5 minutes of grilling.

From apple to mango to tomato, take your pick of the chutney crop. These tangy relishes combine fruits or vegetables with sweet and tart ingredients like honey or vinegar, and spices. The sweet-sour flavor is perfect for broiled chicken.

Green onion fans are a quick but elegant garnish. Just trim onion ends. At the green end, cut 2-inch slits. Place onions in ice water to curl the ends.

Sherry-Sauced Chicken

Total time: 35 minutes

4 chicken thighs *or* 1 whole large chicken breast, halved lengthwise	● Preheat the broiler. Place chicken, skin side down, on an unheated rack in a broiler pan. Broil chicken 4 to 5 inches from the heat for 15 to 18 minutes or till lightly browned on the outside. Turn and broil for 10 to 15 minutes more or till no longer pink.
1 green onion, sliced 1 clove garlic, minced 1 tablespoon butter ¼ cup chicken broth (see tip, page 19) ¼ cup plain yogurt 2 teaspoons all-purpose flour 1 tablespoon chopped pimiento 1 tablespoon dry sherry Paprika	● Meanwhile, in a small saucepan cook onion and garlic in butter till onion is tender but not brown. Add chicken broth. Combine yogurt and flour till smooth and add to saucepan. Cook and stir till mixture is thickened and bubbly. Cook and stir for 1 minute more. Stir in pimiento and sherry. Heat through. Serve over chicken. Sprinkle with paprika. Makes 2 servings.

"Rich-tasting" is the only way to describe this sherry-flavored sauce.

Total time: 25 minutes

Raspberry-Rosé Turkey Steaks

Pictured on pages 4-5.

4 turkey breast tenderloin steaks (about 1 pound) 2 tablespoons butter *or* margarine, melted	● Preheat the broiler. Place turkey on an unheated rack in a broiler pan. Brush with melted butter or margarine. Broil turkey 4 to 5 inches from the heat for 5 minutes. Turn and broil for 4 to 5 minutes more or till no longer pink, brushing occasionally with the remaining butter or margarine.
1 cup frozen unsweetened raspberries ¼ cup rosé wine 1 tablespoon sugar 1 teaspoon cornstarch ⅛ teaspoon ground cinnamon	● Meanwhile, in a blender container or food processor bowl combine raspberries and rosé wine. Cover. Blend well. In a small saucepan combine sugar, cornstarch, and cinnamon. Stir in raspberry mixture. Cook and stir over medium heat till thickened and bubbly. Cook for 2 minutes more. Serve sauce over turkey. Makes 4 servings.
	Grilling directions: Prepare as above, *except* grill turkey on an uncovered grill directly over *medium* coals for 5 minutes. Turn. Grill for 5 to 7 minutes more or till done, brushing often with remaining butter or margarine.

Our taste panel liked the bit of crunch in the sauce from the raspberry seeds. But, if you prefer a smooth sauce and have a little extra time, sieve the blended raspberry mixture.

Cherry-Almond Turkey Steaks

Total time: 30 minutes

4 **turkey breast tenderloin steaks (about 1 pound)**
2 **tablespoons butter** *or* **margarine, melted**

● Preheat the broiler. Place turkey on an unheated rack in a broiler pan. Brush with some of the butter or margarine. Broil turkey 4 to 5 inches from the heat for 4 minutes. Turn and brush with remaining butter or margarine. Broil turkey for 3 to 4 minutes more or till no longer pink. Cover and keep warm.

You'll get rave reviews when you serve this simple but sumptuously sauced turkey.

¼ **cup sliced almonds**
¼ **cup cold water**
2 **teaspoons cornstarch**
⅛ **teaspoon ground cinnamon**
¼ **cup cherry preserves**
1 **drop red food coloring (optional)**

● Meanwhile, in a small skillet cook almonds over medium-low heat about 5 minutes or till the nuts are toasted, stirring constantly.
   For sauce, in a small saucepan combine water, cornstarch, and cinnamon. Stir in cherry preserves and food coloring, if desired. Cook and stir over medium heat till mixture is thickened and bubbly. Cook and stir for 1 minute more.

1 **cup frozen unsweetened pitted, tart red cherries**

● Stir in frozen cherries. Cook till cherries are thawed and sauce is heated through, stirring occasionally. Spoon some of the sauce over turkey. Sprinkle with the toasted almonds. Pass remaining sauce. Makes 4 servings.

Grilling directions: Prepare as above, *except* grill turkey on an uncovered grill directly over *medium* coals for 5 minutes. Turn and grill for 5 to 7 minutes more or till done.

Spice-of-Life Kabobs

Total time: 35 minutes

½ cup apricot preserves
2 tablespoons dry white wine
¼ teaspoon ground allspice

2 whole large skinned and boned chicken breasts, cut into 2 x½-inch strips
2 small zucchini, cut into ½-inch slices
1 large sweet red *or* green pepper, cut into 1-inch pieces
8 cherry tomatoes

● For glaze, in a small saucepan stir together apricot preserves, white wine, and allspice. Cook, stirring occasionally, till heated through.

● Meanwhile, preheat the broiler. Thread chicken onto 8 skewers alternately with zucchini and pepper (see photo, below). Brush with glaze mixture.

Place skewers on an unheated rack in a broiler pan. Broil 4 inches from the heat for 3 to 4 minutes or till lightly browned. Turn and brush with glaze mixture. Broil for 3 to 4 minutes more or till chicken is no longer pink and vegetables are of desired doneness. Put a cherry tomato on the end of each skewer and broil for 1 minute more. Pass sauce. Makes 4 servings.

Grilling directions: Prepare as above, *except* grill kabobs on an uncovered grill directly over *medium-hot* coals for 8 to 10 minutes or till chicken is no longer pink and vegetables are tender, turning once and brushing often with the glaze. Add tomatoes. Grill for 1 minute more.

Put a little zest in your next meal when you feature these kabobs as the main attraction. The slightly spicy, sweet glaze is a wonderful complement to chicken and vegetables.

Thread the chicken onto the skewers by folding the pieces in half.

Total time: 25 minutes

French Bread Pizza

1 15-ounce can pizza sauce 8 ounces turkey ham, cut into bite-size strips ½ teaspoon dried oregano, crushed ⅛ teaspoon garlic powder	● Preheat the broiler. Meanwhile, in a medium saucepan combine pizza sauce, turkey ham, oregano, and garlic powder. Cook, covered, over medium heat for 4 to 5 minutes or till mixture is heated through, stirring occasionally.
1 16-ounce loaf unsliced French bread (14 to 16 inches long) 1 12-ounce package shredded mozzarella cheese (3 cups)	● Slice French bread in half horizontally. Hollow out each half, leaving a ½- to ¾-inch shell. Place bread halves, cut side up, on a baking sheet. Sprinkle ¼ of the cheese atop each bread half. Broil 4 to 5 inches from the heat for 2 to 4 minutes or just till cheese is melted.
1 small green pepper, cut into rings	● Spoon pizza sauce mixture into bread halves. Sprinkle with the remaining cheese and top with green pepper rings. Broil for 2 to 3 minutes or till cheese is melted and bubbly. Serve immediately. Makes 4 to 6 servings.

French bread "boats" make perfect crusts for these quick turkey ham and cheese pizzas.

Give Grilling A Go

Though grilling takes a little longer than cooking under the broiler, it's still a fun, flavorful, and convenient way to cook. Here are some tips to make cooking over the coals quicker and easier:
● Spray the cold grill rack with a nonstick spray coating before cooking to make washing a whiz.
● Streamline cooking time by putting your food on to cook when the coals are at just the right temperature. To determine the temperature of the coals, hold the palm of your hand above the coals at the height your food will be cooked and count the seconds (by saying "one thousand one," and so forth). If you have to remove your hand after three seconds, the coals are *medium-hot;* after four seconds, they're *medium.*
● Speed cleanup by lining the firebox with *heavy* foil. When you're done and the ashes are cooled, just fold up the foil and toss it.

Currant Barbecue-Style Chicken

Total time: 40 minutes

2 to 2½ pounds meaty chicken pieces (breasts, wings, thighs, and drumsticks)	● Preheat the broiler. Place chicken pieces, skin side down, on an unheated rack in a broiler pan. Broil 4 to 5 inches from the heat for 15 to 18 minutes or till chicken is lightly browned.
¼ cup currant jelly **¼ cup chili sauce** **1 tablespoon soy sauce** **1 tablespoon vinegar** **⅛ teaspoon garlic powder** **Several drops bottled hot pepper sauce**	● Meanwhile, for sauce, in a small saucepan stir together jelly, chili sauce, soy sauce, vinegar, garlic powder, and hot pepper sauce. Cook over medium-low heat for 10 to 12 minutes or till bubbly, stirring occasionally to melt jelly.
1 orange, sliced (optional) **Fresh parsley (optional)**	● Brush chicken pieces with some of the sauce. Turn and broil for 10 to 15 minutes more or till chicken is no longer pink. Brush with sauce. Garnish with orange slices and parsley, if desired, and pass remaining sauce. Makes 4 servings.

To grill chicken, prepare as directed, *except* grill the pieces, skin side down, on an uncovered grill directly over *medium* coals for 20 minutes. Turn the pieces. Brush with sauce. Grill for 10 to 20 minutes more or till done. Brush with sauce.

Quick Cooked Chicken

Don't worry if you haven't any leftover cooked chicken to cut up. Here are two ways to turn 2 whole medium chicken breasts, halved lengthwise (about 1½ pounds), *or* ¾ pound skinned and boned chicken breasts into about 2 cups of cubed, cooked chicken:
● Micro-cook the chicken in a 1½-quart nonmetal casserole, covered, on 100% power (high) for 8 to 9 minutes (4 to 5 minutes for boneless pieces) or till no longer pink, turning the pieces once.
● Poach the chicken in a 10-inch skillet in 1⅓ cups boiling water. Simmer, covered, for 18 to 20 minutes (12 to 14 minutes for boneless pieces) or till done.
● P.S. If you're really rushed for time, use packaged frozen cubed cooked chicken (be sure to use generous cup measurements).

Total time: 25 minutes

Fruit-Sauced Turkey Patties

1	beaten egg
½	cup soft bread crumbs
4	green onions, thinly sliced
½	teaspoon salt
¼	teaspoon dried marjoram, crushed
¼	teaspoon dried savory, crushed
¼	teaspoon pepper
1	pound ground raw turkey

● Preheat the broiler. In a medium mixing bowl stir together egg, bread crumbs, green onions, salt, marjoram, savory, and pepper. Add ground turkey. Mix well.

Shape meat mixture into four ½-inch-thick patties. Place patties on an unheated rack in a broiler pan. Broil 3 to 4 inches from the heat for 5 minutes. Turn patties and broil for 4 to 5 minutes or till no longer pink.

This naturally light and lean recipe is great whether you're watching your weight or not.

1	5½-ounce can apricot nectar
⅓	cup mixed dried fruit bits
¼	cup orange juice
2	teaspoons cornstarch
	Hot cooked noodles (optional)

● Meanwhile, for sauce, in a small saucepan stir apricot nectar, fruit bits, and orange juice into cornstarch. Cook and stir till mixture is thickened and bubbly. Cook and stir for 2 minutes more. Serve sauce and patties with hot cooked noodles, if desired. Serves 4.

Grilling directions: Prepare as above, *except* grill patties on an uncovered grill directly over *medium* coals for 5 minutes. Turn patties and grill for 4 to 5 minutes more or till done.

Total time: 25 minutes

Teriyaki Turkey Patties

1	beaten egg
½	cup soft bread crumbs
¼	cup chopped water chestnuts
2	green onions, sliced
1	tablespoon teriyaki sauce
1	pound ground raw turkey

● Preheat the broiler. In a medium mixing bowl combine the beaten egg, bread crumbs, water chestnuts, green onions, and teriyaki sauce. Add ground turkey. Mix well.

Shape meat mixture into four ½-inch-thick patties. Place patties on a lightly greased unheated rack in a broiler pan. Broil 3 to 4 inches from the heat for 5 minutes. Turn patties and broil for 4 to 5 minutes more or till no longer pink.

Burger buffs will enjoy the tang and texture of these savory Oriental-style turkey patties.

⅓	cup orange marmalade
1	tablespoon teriyaki sauce
½	teaspoon sesame seed

● Meanwhile, for sauce, in a saucepan stir together orange marmalade, teriyaki sauce, and sesame seed. Cook over medium-low heat just till marmalade is melted, stirring occasionally. Serve patties with sauce. Makes 4 servings.

Total time: 25 minutes

Chili Nugget Nibbles

¼ cup cornmeal
1 teaspoon chili powder
¼ teaspoon garlic salt
¼ teaspoon pepper
¼ teaspoon ground red
    pepper
2 whole medium skinned
    and boned chicken
    breasts, cut into 1-inch
    pieces (about 1 pound)
2 tablespoons butter *or*
    margarine, melted

● In a plastic bag combine cornmeal, chili powder, garlic salt, pepper, and red pepper. Coat chicken pieces with melted butter or margarine. Put pieces into bag. Close bag and shake to coat chicken.

Place chicken pieces in a single layer on a baking sheet. Bake in a 400° oven for 8 to 10 minutes or till no longer pink, turning pieces once.

Whether you serve them for dinner, or as fun finger food at your next party, you'll discover these nuggets are worth their weight in gold.

½ cup dairy sour cream
2 tablespoons chopped
    green chili peppers

● Meanwhile, for dipping sauce, in a small bowl stir together the sour cream and chopped green chili peppers. Serve chicken with dipping sauce. Serves 4.

Turkey-Pastrami Pizza

Total time: 35 minutes

1¼ cups packaged biscuit mix
¼ teaspoon caraway seed
¼ cup cold water

● In a medium mixing bowl stir together biscuit mix and caraway seed. Add water and stir till moistened. Pat the dough onto a greased 12-inch pizza pan (see photo, below).

1 8-ounce can sauerkraut, rinsed and drained well (1 cup)
¼ cup Thousand Island salad dressing
6 ounces sliced Swiss cheese
1 8-ounce package turkey pastrami, cut into 1-inch pieces

● In a small mixing bowl stir together the sauerkraut and salad dressing. Arrange *half* of the cheese on the prepared dough, tearing cheese to fit. Arrange the turkey atop the cheese. Spoon the sauerkraut mixture over all. Top with remaining cheese. Bake in a 425° oven about 15 minutes or till bubbly. Cut into pieces to serve. Makes 4 to 6 servings.

Even sauerkraut snubbers won't be able to pass up this pastrami pizza. For pure pizza pleasure, rinse the sauerkraut to remove much of the salt and harshness.

Pat the dough as evenly as possible onto the bottom and partway up the sides of the pizza pan.

Curried Chicken and Broccoli

Total time: 35 minutes

1 **10-ounce package frozen cut broccoli**
1 **11-ounce can condensed cheddar cheese soup**
⅓ **cup mayonnaise *or* salad dressing**
2 **tablespoons milk**
1½ **to 2 teaspoons curry powder**
2 **teaspoons lemon juice**

● In a saucepan add broccoli to ½ cup boiling *water*. Return to boiling. Cook, uncovered, for 4 minutes. Drain.

Meanwhile, for cheese sauce, in a medium mixing bowl stir together soup, mayonnaise or salad dressing, milk, curry powder, and lemon juice.

Don't be a chicken! Dare to dress up leftover chicken with broccoli and a rich curry sauce for an entrée that's elegant enough for company.

1½ **cups cubed cooked chicken**
½ **of an 8-ounce can (½ cup) sliced water chestnuts, drained**
¼ **cup chopped cashews *or* peanuts**

● Evenly divide the broccoli between 4 individual au gratin dishes. Top *each* dish with ¼ of the chicken and water chestnuts. Spoon ¼ of the cheese sauce over each dish. Top with chopped cashews or peanuts. Bake, uncovered, in a 375° oven for 12 to 15 minutes or till heated through. Makes 4 servings.

Microwave directions: In a 1-quart nonmetal casserole micro-cook broccoli, covered, in 2 tablespoons *water* on 100% power (high) for 4 minutes. Prepare cheese sauce as above. Fill 4 nonmetal individual au gratin dishes as above. Micro-cook, uncovered, for 6 to 8 minutes or till heated through, giving dishes a half-turn and rearranging once.

Take Stock!

It's tough to top the taste of homemade chicken broth, but don't despair if you haven't the time to prepare it. Here are several options. When a recipe calls for chicken broth, use instant bouillon granules or cubes mixed with water according to package directions. Or, opt for canned broths. Regular broth is ready to use straight from the can, but dilute *condensed* broth according to can directions.

Pecan Hollandaise-Sauced Turkey

Total time: 30 minutes

1 **11-ounce package frozen long grain and wild rice**
1 **10-ounce package frozen asparagus spears**
4 **turkey breast slices (about ¾ pound)**

● Prepare rice according to package directions. Meanwhile, cook asparagus in a small amount of boiling water for 5 to 7 minutes or till crisp-tender. Drain. Put ¼ of the asparagus spears crosswise onto *each* turkey slice. Roll up slices.

1 **tablespoon butter *or* margarine, melted**
⅛ **teaspoon garlic salt**

● Place turkey rolls, seam side down, in a greased 8x8x2-inch baking dish. Mix butter and garlic salt. Brush over turkey rolls. Bake in a 375° oven for 13 to 15 minutes or till turkey is no longer pink. Keep warm.

¼ **cup pecan pieces**
2 **egg yolks**
2 **tablespoons water**

● Meanwhile, for pecan hollandaise, place pecans in a blender container. Cover. Blend till nuts are finely ground. Add egg yolks and water. Cover. Blend about 5 seconds or till mixed.

6 **tablespoons butter *or* margarine**
1 **tablespoon lemon juice Pecan halves (optional)**

● In a small saucepan heat butter and lemon juice till butter is melted and almost boiling. With blender lid ajar and blender running at high speed, slowly pour in butter mixture. Continue to blend about 30 seconds more or till thick and fluffy (if necessary, stir in about 1 tablespoon hot *water* for desired consistency). Serve immediately over turkey rolls and rice. Top with a pecan half, if desired. Makes 4 servings.

Microwave directions: Prepare rice according to package directions. In an 8x8x2-inch nonmetal baking dish combine asparagus and 2 tablespoons *water*. Micro-cook, covered with vented plastic wrap, on 100% power (high) for 4 to 6 minutes or just till asparagus is tender, stirring once. Drain.

Assemble turkey rolls as above. In a 6-ounce custard cup combine butter and garlic salt. Cook, uncovered, for 30 to 60 seconds or till butter is melted. Brush over turkey rolls. Cook, covered with vented plastic wrap, for 4 to 6 minutes or till turkey is no longer pink, rearranging turkey rolls and giving dish a half-turn once. Keep warm.

Prepare pecan hollandaise as above, *except* in a 1-cup glass measure cook butter and lemon juice for 1 to 1½ minutes or till melted. Serve as above.

Dine in instead of out tonight. It will give you the chance to savor the delicate blend of flavors of this gourmet fare, and you won't even have to leave a tip!

Golden-Crusted Chicken Pies

Total time: 30 minutes

1 tablespoon all-purpose
   flour
1 10¾-ounce can chunky
   vegetable soup
¼ cup milk
¼ teaspoon pepper
1½ cups cubed cooked
   chicken *or* turkey
1 3-ounce package cream
   cheese, cubed

● In a medium saucepan stir flour into soup. Stir in milk and pepper. Cook and stir over medium heat till mixture is thickened and bubbly. Cook for 1 minute more. Stir in chicken or turkey and cream cheese. Heat through, stirring to melt cream cheese.

When is a can of soup *not* just a can of soup? When you turn it into the creamy base for these palate-pleasin' pot pies.

1 package (6) refrigerated
   buttermilk *or* country-
   style biscuits

● Pour the hot chicken mixture into three 10-ounce custard cups. Separate the biscuits and arrange *2* biscuits atop *each* custard cup. Bake in a 375° oven for 12 to 15 minutes or till biscuits are golden brown. Makes 3 servings.

Cutting Costs to The Bone

Although timesaving skinned and boned chicken breasts are readily available in most supermarkets, you can often save money by doing the work yourself. Here's a super-simple way.

1. Place the chicken breast, skin side up, on a cutting board. Pull the skin away from the meat and discard it.

2. Using a thin sharp knife and a sawing motion, begin cutting on one side of the breastbone. Cut as close to the bone as possible and gently pull the meat away from the bone, as shown.

Florentine Chicken

Total time: 45 minutes

1 12-ounce package frozen spinach soufflé	● Run warm water over spinach soufflé for a few seconds to loosen it from pan. Remove soufflé from pan and divide it into 4 squares.
2 whole medium skinned and boned chicken breasts, halved lengthwise	● Place a chicken breast half, boned side up, between 2 pieces of clear plastic wrap. Working from the center to the edges, pound the chicken lightly with the fine-toothed or flat side of a meat mallet to a ¼-inch thickness (see photo, page 26). Repeat with remaining chicken.
1 4-ounce can sliced mushrooms, drained	● Place chicken pieces in a greased 13x9x2-inch baking dish. Top *each* piece with some of the mushrooms and *1 square* of spinach soufflé. Bake in a 400° oven for 20 minutes.
½ cup shredded cheddar cheese (2 ounces)	● Sprinkle ¼ of the shredded cheese atop *each* piece and bake for about 5 minutes more or till the chicken is no longer pink and the soufflé is heated through. Makes 4 servings.

In a jiffy, turn a side dish heat-and-serve spinach soufflé into an easy, elegant entrée.

Mama's Little Dumplings

Total time: 30 minutes

1	10-ounce package frozen peas and carrots
2	medium parsnips, sliced
1½	cups chicken broth (see tip, page 19)

● In a large saucepan combine peas and carrots, parsnips, and chicken broth. Bring to boiling. Reduce the heat. Simmer, covered, for 6 minutes or till vegetables are crisp-tender.

½	cup chicken broth
2	tablespoons all-purpose flour
2	cups cubed cooked chicken
2	teaspoons dried minced onion
1	teaspoon dried dillweed

● Stir together chicken broth and flour till smooth. Stir into vegetable mixture. Add chicken, onion, dillweed, and ¼ teaspoon *pepper*. Bring to boiling. Reduce the heat. Cook and stir till thickened and bubbly.

½	cup all-purpose flour
¼	cup shredded cheddar cheese (1 ounce)
¾	teaspoon baking powder
½	teaspoon dried parsley flakes *or* 2 teaspoons snipped parsley
¼	cup milk
1	tablespoon cooking oil

● In a small bowl stir together the flour, cheese, baking powder, parsley, and dash *salt*. Add milk and oil all at once. Stir just till moistened. Drop the dough into 4 mounds atop the bubbling chicken mixture. Cover tightly and simmer for 8 minutes or till a toothpick inserted in a dumpling comes out clean. Serves 4.

Chicken and dumplings get a new lease on life when you can have them on the table in half an hour. Now even on the busiest days, your family can savor the goodness of this robust classic.

Creole Chicken

Total time: 30 minutes

⅔ cup long grain rice
1 small onion, finely chopped (¼ cup)
¼ cup finely chopped green pepper
2 tablespoons butter *or* margarine
1 8-ounce can tomato sauce
1 4-ounce can mushroom stems and pieces, drained
½ teaspoon sugar
¼ to ½ teaspoon bottled hot pepper sauce
1 bay leaf

● Cook rice according to package directions. Meanwhile, in a large skillet cook onion and green pepper in butter or margarine till vegetables are tender but not brown. Stir in tomato sauce, mushrooms, sugar, hot pepper sauce, and bay leaf. Bring to boiling. Reduce the heat. Cook, uncovered, over medium-low heat for 5 minutes. Remove bay leaf.

Bring some of the charm of the Deep South to your table whenever you serve this spicy one-dish meal. It's inspired by the melting-pot cooking of old New Orleans.

2 whole large skinned and boned chicken breasts, halved lengthwise

● Meanwhile, place *each* chicken breast half, boned side up, between 2 pieces of clear plastic wrap. Working from the center to the edges, pound the chicken lightly with the fine-toothed or flat side of a meat mallet to ¼-inch thickness (see photo, below). Remove the plastic wrap. Place chicken pieces in the skillet. Spoon sauce over pieces. Cook, covered, over medium heat for 5 to 7 minutes or till meat is no longer pink. Serve over rice. Makes 4 servings.

Place the chicken piece between two pieces of clear plastic wrap and use the fine-toothed or flat side of a meat mallet to lightly pound the meat to the desired thickness.

Total time: 25 minutes

Turkey Stroganoff

| 2 | cups wide noodles (4 ounces) | ● Cook noodles according to package directions. Drain. Set aside. |

Sauces cooked in the microwave don't evaporate the same way they do on the range top. So, you'll need to cut the water a little when you make this recipe in the microwave oven.

1	pound ground raw turkey
8	ounces fresh mushrooms, sliced (3 cups)
1	medium onion, chopped
1	teaspoon instant chicken bouillon granules
½	teaspoon dried thyme, crushed
½	teaspoon garlic salt
⅛	teaspoon ground nutmeg

● Meanwhile, in a 12-inch skillet cook ground turkey, mushrooms, and onion over medium heat till turkey is no longer pink and onion is tender but not brown, stirring occasionally to break up turkey. Stir in ¾ cup *water,* bouillon granules, thyme, garlic salt, and nutmeg.

| 3 | tablespoons all-purpose flour |
| 1 | 8-ounce carton dairy sour cream *or* plain yogurt
Paprika (optional) |

● In a small mixing bowl stir flour into sour cream or yogurt till smooth. Stir into skillet. Cook and stir over medium heat till thickened and bubbly. Cook for 1 minute more. Serve over noodles. Sprinkle with paprika, if desired. Makes 4 servings.

Microwave Directions: Cook noodles as above. In a 2-quart nonmetal casserole, crumble the ground turkey. Micro-cook turkey, mushrooms, and onion, uncovered, on 100% power (high) for 7 to 10 minutes or till turkey is no longer pink and vegetables are tender, stirring twice. Stir in ⅔ *cup* water, bouillon granules, thyme, garlic salt, and nutmeg. In a small bowl stir the flour into the sour cream till smooth. Stir into turkey mixture. Cook, uncovered, for 7 to 10 minutes or till thickened and bubbly, stirring every 2 minutes. Cook for 30 seconds more. Serve as above.

Total time: 20 minutes

Chicken Shortcakes

1	cup frozen peas and carrots
1	11-ounce can condensed cheddar cheese soup
¼	cup milk Several dashes bottled hot pepper sauce
1½	cups cubed cooked chicken

● In a medium saucepan cook the vegetables, covered, in ¼ cup *boiling water* for 5 minutes. Drain. Set aside.
In the same saucepan stir together soup, milk, and hot pepper sauce. Add chicken and cooked vegetables. Cook over medium heat about 10 minutes or till heated through, stirring occasionally.

We could have called this jiffy-quick chicken dish "Chicken Shortcuts" since it's only 20 minutes from start to finish. By either name, it tastes great—a surefire hit with kids, too.

| 6 | rusks *or* 3 English muffins, split and toasted |

● To serve, place *2* rusks or toasted English muffin halves on *each* of *3* dinner plates. Spoon chicken mixture over rusks or muffin halves. Serves 3.

Total time: 25 minutes

Creamy Chicken and Broccoli

4 eggs
1 10-ounce package frozen broccoli *or* asparagus spears

● Place eggs in a small saucepan. Add *warm* water to cover. Bring to boiling over high heat. Reduce the heat. Simmer, covered, for 15 minutes. Pour off hot water. Fill saucepan with *cold* water. Let stand for 2 minutes. Peel and slice eggs.

Meanwhile, cook broccoli or asparagus spears according to package directions. Drain well. Keep warm.

2 tablespoons butter *or* margarine
¼ cup slivered almonds
2 tablespoons all-purpose flour
1 teaspoon instant chicken bouillon granules
¼ teaspoon salt
⅛ teaspoon pepper
1 cup milk
1½ cups cubed cooked chicken
8 rusks
Snipped parsley

● In a medium saucepan melt butter over medium heat. Add almonds. Cook, stirring occasionally, till nuts are toasted. Stir in the flour, bouillon granules, salt, and pepper. Add milk all at once. Cook and stir over medium heat till thickened and bubbly. Cook and stir for 1 minute more. Stir in the chicken. Heat through.

For each serving, place ¼ of the broccoli over *2* rusks. Spoon ¼ of the chicken mixture atop. Top with some of the egg slices and parsley. Serves 4.

If you find the sauce for this upscale creamed chicken on rusks a bit thick, thin it slightly by adding one or two tablespoons more milk.

Sweet 'n' Sour Skillet Burgers

Total time: 35 minutes

4 ounces wide noodles (3 cups)

● Cook noodles according to package directions. Drain.

1 beaten egg
¼ cup fine dry bread crumbs
¼ cup raisins
2 teaspoons dried minced onion
1 pound ground raw turkey
1 tablespoon cooking oil

● Meanwhile, in a large bowl combine egg, bread crumbs, raisins, onion, and ¼ teaspoon *salt*. Add ground turkey. Mix well. Shape meat mixture into four ¾-inch-thick patties. In a 10-inch skillet cook patties in hot oil over medium heat for 5 minutes, turning once. Drain.

1 8-ounce can tomato sauce
⅔ cup apple cider *or* juice
1 teaspoon brown sugar
¼ teaspoon dry mustard
Dash ground cloves

● For sauce, mix tomato sauce, apple cider or juice, brown sugar, mustard, and cloves. Pour over burgers in skillet. Cook, covered, over medium-low heat for 8 to 10 minutes or till meat is no longer pink. Remove burgers. Keep warm.

2 gingersnaps, finely crushed (2 tablespoons)

● Stir gingersnaps into sauce. Cook and stir 1 to 2 minutes or till bubbly. Serve burgers over noodles with some of the sauce. Pass remaining sauce. Serves 4.

Styled after German sauerbraten, these burgers have a delightfully different sweet and sour flavor. The crushed gingersnaps add a hint of sweetness and help thicken the sauce as well.

Creamy Chicken and Broccoli

Orange-Papaya Chicken

Pictured on pages 4-5.

Total time: 30 minutes

1½ teaspoons cornstarch
½ teaspoon finely shredded orange peel
½ teaspoon ground ginger
⅛ teaspoon salt
½ cup orange juice
1 teaspoon honey
2 whole large skinned and boned chicken breasts, halved lengthwise

● For sauce, in a small saucepan combine cornstarch, orange peel, ginger, and salt. Stir in orange juice and honey. Set aside.
  Place *each* chicken breast half, boned side up, between 2 pieces of clear plastic wrap. Working from the center to the edges, pound the chicken lightly with the fine-toothed or flat side of a meat mallet to a ¼-inch thickness (see photo, page 26). Remove plastic wrap.

Elegantly laced with papaya and garnished with kiwi fruit, this acclaimed fruity-sauced chicken is sure to bring down the house.

1 tablespoon cooking oil
1 tablespoon butter *or* margarine

● In a 10-inch skillet cook chicken, 2 pieces at a time, in hot oil and butter over medium heat for 2 minutes. Turn and cook for 1 to 2 minutes more or till no longer pink. Transfer chicken to a serving platter. Cover. Keep warm.

1 medium papaya, peeled, seeded, and cut up, *or* one 8-ounce can chunk pineapple, drained
1 tablespoon butter *or* margarine
  Kiwi fruit, peeled and sliced
  Hot cooked rice (optional)

● Meanwhile, cook and stir sauce over medium heat till thickened and bubbly. Cook and stir for 2 minutes more. Stir in papaya or pineapple and butter or margarine. Heat through. Spoon sauce over chicken. Garnish with kiwi fruit and serve with hot cooked rice, if desired. Makes 4 servings.

Speedy Spaghetti

Total time: 30 minutes

1 pound ground raw turkey
1 medium onion, chopped
2 cloves garlic, minced, *or* ¼ teaspoon garlic powder
¼ teaspoon pepper

● In a 3-quart saucepan cook and stir ground turkey, onion, garlic or garlic powder, and pepper over medium heat till the turkey is no longer pink and the onion is tender.

When only homemade spaghetti will do, but time is running out, pull this ace from up your sleeve. Everyone will love it.

2½ cups chicken broth (see tip, page 19)
1 6-ounce can Italian-style *or* regular-style tomato paste
1 2½-ounce can sliced mushrooms, drained
¼ teaspoon fennel seed, crushed
6 ounces spaghetti, broken
  Parmesan cheese

● Stir in chicken broth, tomato paste, mushrooms, and fennel seed. Bring mixture to boiling. Add spaghetti, a little at a time, stirring well. Cook, covered, over medium-low heat for 12 to 15 minutes or till spaghetti is tender, stirring frequently. Sprinkle each serving with Parmesan cheese. Makes 4 servings.

Cider Chicken with Mushrooms

Total time: 30 minutes

1 whole large skinned and boned chicken breast, halved lengthwise
1 medium apple, cored and sliced
½ cup sliced fresh mushrooms
2 tablespoons butter *or* margarine

● In a 10-inch skillet cook chicken, apple, and mushrooms in butter or margarine, covered, over medium heat for 8 to 10 minutes or till chicken is lightly browned on the outside and no longer pink, turning once. Remove chicken, apple, and mushrooms from skillet with slotted spoon, reserving the pan juices. Keep warm.

1 teaspoon cornstarch
⅛ teaspoon ground allspice
Dash paprika (optional)
⅓ cup apple cider *or* apple juice

● For sauce, stir together cornstarch, allspice, and paprika, if desired. Stir in apple cider or juice. Stir into reserved juices in skillet. Cook and stir over medium heat till mixture is thickened and bubbly. Cook and stir for 2 minutes more. Spoon the sauce over the chicken, apple, and mushrooms. Serves 2.

Whether you buy it in a can or a jar, apple cider and apple juice by any name will perform the same.

Turkey and Eggplant Italiano

Total time: 30 minutes

1 beaten egg
¼ cup seasoned fine dry bread crumbs
2 tablespoons milk
¼ teaspoon garlic salt
1 pound ground raw turkey
2 tablespoons cooking oil

● In a medium mixing bowl stir together egg, bread crumbs, milk, and garlic salt. Add ground turkey. Mix well. Shape mixture into four ¾-inch-thick patties.

  In a 10-inch skillet, cook patties in hot cooking oil for 10 minutes or till lightly browned on the outside and no longer pink, turning once. Remove from the skillet. Drain.

1 15½-ounce jar chunky garden-style spaghetti sauce
1 small eggplant, cut into ½-inch cubes
1 4-ounce package shredded mozzarella cheese (1 cup)

● Pour spaghetti sauce into skillet. Add eggplant pieces. Cook, covered, over medium heat for 6 minutes or till eggplant is tender, stirring often. Top with turkey patties and cheese. Cook, covered, for 1 to 2 minutes more or till patties are warm and cheese is melted. Makes 4 servings.

Any meatless, thick-style spaghetti sauce will taste *delizioso* in this Italian-style dish—try a different one each time!

Campaign-Spirit Chicken

Total time: 30 minutes

2 tablespoons butter *or* margarine
2 whole large skinned and boned chicken breasts, halved lengthwise
½ pound small, whole mushrooms, halved
⅔ cup champagne *or* dry white wine
¼ teaspoon salt
¼ teaspoon dried tarragon, crushed
⅛ teaspoon pepper

● In a 10-inch skillet melt butter or margarine. Add chicken and cook over medium high heat for 5 to 7 minutes or till lightly browned on both sides. Reduce the heat. Add mushrooms, champagne or white wine, salt, tarragon, and pepper. Cook, covered, over medium heat about 15 minutes or till the chicken is no longer pink.

With support for chicken at an all-time high among kitchen constituents, the popular vote is sure to keep this impressively qualified candidate on your mealtime ballot.

¼ cup light cream *or* milk
1 tablespoon cornstarch

● Meanwhile, in a small mixing bowl stir together cream or milk and cornstarch. Remove chicken and mushrooms from skillet, reserving liquid (about ½ cup). Keep chicken and mushrooms warm.
    Stir cream mixture into reserved liquid in skillet. Cook and stir till thickened and bubbly. Cook and stir for 1 minute more. Spoon over chicken and mushrooms. Makes 4 servings.

Wheat Berry-Vegetable Pilaf

Total time: 40 minutes

¼ cup soft wheat berries
1 cup hot water

● In a small saucepan combine wheat berries and water. Bring to boiling. Reduce the heat. Cook, covered, over medium heat for 15 minutes. Drain.

Wheat berries add a crunchy wholesomeness that helps make this main-dish pilaf just a bit different. If soft wheat berries are not available, you can use hard wheat berries but soak them overnight in the hot water before cooking.

2 whole medium skinned and boned chicken breasts
1 medium onion, chopped
1 tablespoon cooking oil
½ to 1 teaspoon curry powder

● Meanwhile, cut chicken into 1½-inch pieces. In a 10-inch skillet cook chicken and onion in hot oil about 4 minutes or till chicken is no longer pink and onion is tender. Add curry powder and cook for 1 minute more. Remove chicken and onion from skillet. Set aside.

1½ cups chicken broth (see tip, page 19)
1 cup quick-cooking brown rice

● In the same skillet combine wheat berries, chicken broth, and rice. Bring mixture to boiling. Reduce the heat. Simmer, covered, over medium-low heat for 6 minutes.

1½ cups loose-pack frozen mixed vegetables

● Add vegetables and return to boiling. Reduce the heat. Cook, covered, for 6 minutes more or till vegetables and rice are tender. Add chicken and onion. Heat through. Makes 4 servings.

Wheat berries (unpolished whole wheat kernels) are readily available at health food stores.

Pizza-Sauced Zucchini Chicken

Total time: 30 minutes

3 small zucchini, cut into ¼-inch slices (3 cups)

● In a medium saucepan cook zucchini, covered, in a small amount of boiling water for 4 to 6 minutes or till crisp-tender. Drain well.

⅓ cup fine dry seasoned bread crumbs
2 tablespoons Parmesan cheese
2 whole large skinned and boned chicken breasts, halved lengthwise
1 beaten egg
1 tablespoon cooking oil

● Meanwhile, in a shallow dish stir together the bread crumbs and Parmesan cheese. Dip breast halves into egg and then into bread crumb mixture.
  In a 10-inch skillet cook chicken in hot oil for 6 to 8 minutes or till lightly browned on the outside and no longer pink, turning once. Drain well.

1 8-ounce can pizza sauce
½ of a 4-ounce package shredded mozzarella cheese (½ cup)

● Arrange zucchini in skillet around and atop chicken pieces. Pour pizza sauce over all. Cook, covered, for 4 to 6 minutes or till heated through. Sprinkle cheese over chicken pieces. Let stand for 1 minute before serving. Serves 4.

The chicken pieces in this dish are coated with a mixture of seasoned bread crumbs and Parmesan cheese, much like veal Parmigiana. In fact, you get a very similar taste in just a fraction of the time.

Apricot-Cardamom Drumsticks

Total time: 45 minutes

1 8¾-ounce can unpeeled apricot halves

● Drain apricots, reserving ¼ *cup* of the liquid. Cut apricots into ½-inch pieces.

8 chicken drumsticks (about 1¾ pounds)
1 tablespoon cooking oil
¼ cup water
2 teaspoons dried minced onion
¼ teaspoon ground cardamom *or* ½ teaspoon ground coriander
½ teaspoon instant chicken bouillon granules
¼ teaspoon salt
⅛ teaspoon garlic powder
⅛ teaspoon pepper
1 cup ready-to-cook couscous *or* long grain rice

● In a 10-inch skillet brown chicken on all sides in hot cooking oil. Drain. Add reserved apricot juice, water, onion, cardamom or coriander, bouillon granules, salt, garlic powder, and pepper. Cook, covered, over medium-low heat for 20 to 25 minutes or till chicken is no longer pink.
  Meanwhile, cook couscous or rice according to package directions. Stir apricots into the cooked couscous or rice. Spoon onto a serving platter. With tongs, remove chicken from skillet and place atop couscous or rice mixture. Skim fat from pan juices. Spoon pan juices over chicken and couscous or rice. Makes 4 servings.

Couscous (COO-skoos), traditionally a North African or Middle Eastern side dish, isn't as exotic as it sounds. It is a farina-like product you can use as you would rice.

King Hank's PDQ-BBQ Turkey

Total time: 25 minutes

½ cup catsup
2 tablespoons brown sugar
2 tablespoons water
1 tablespoon vinegar
1 teaspoon Worcestershire sauce
¼ teaspoon crushed red pepper
¼ teaspoon ground cinnamon

● For sauce, in a 2-cup measure stir together catsup, brown sugar, water, vinegar, Worcestershire sauce, red pepper, and cinnamon. Micro-cook, uncovered, on 100% power (high) for 1½ to 2½ minutes or till bubbly, stirring once. Set mixture aside.

2 turkey drumsticks (about 1 pound each) *or* 2 to 2½ pounds meaty chicken pieces (breasts, wings, thighs, and drumsticks)

● In a 12x7x2-inch nonmetal baking dish arrange turkey or chicken pieces, skin side down, with meatiest portions toward the outside (see photo, page 38). Cook, loosely covered with waxed paper, on high for 8 minutes, giving dish a half-turn once. (Note: If using turkey, shield ends of drumsticks with foil, provided the owner's manual permits the use of metal in your particular microwave oven.) Drain well.

● Brush turkey or chicken with sauce. Turn and brush again. Cook, covered loosely with waxed paper, on high for 6 to 8 minutes more or till turkey is no longer pink (4 to 6 minutes for chicken). Remove baking dish from oven. Keep warm. Cook remaining sauce, uncovered, for 1 to 2 minutes or till hot. Pass with turkey or chicken. Makes 4 servings.

Micro-Plus Grilled Chicken: Prepare chicken as above, *except* after cooking for 8 minutes, transfer to a preheated grill. Arrange chicken, skin side down, directly over *medium* coals. Brush with sauce. Grill for 5 minutes. Turn. Brush with sauce. Grill for 6 to 8 minutes more or till done, brushing often with sauce.

Wheat 'n' Nut Chicken

Total time: 30 minutes

⅓ cup ground walnuts *or* pecans
2 tablespoons wheat germ
1 tablespoon all-purpose flour
¼ teaspoon salt
¼ teaspoon pepper

● In a shallow dish or pie plate stir together ground walnuts or pecans, wheat germ, flour, salt, and pepper.

Soggy chicken puts a damper on any meal, so our Test Kitchen developed a new way to crisp-cook coated chicken in the microwave oven. To keep the coating crisp, coat only three sides of the chicken pieces and cook them, uncoated side down, on a nonmetal rack.

2 to 2½ pounds meaty chicken pieces (breasts, wings, thighs, and drumsticks)
1 tablespoon milk

● On waxed paper brush each chicken piece with milk. Roll pieces in nut mixture to coat on *3* sides.

● In a 12x7½x2-inch nonmetal baking dish arrange pieces on a nonmetal rack with *uncoated* side down and the meatiest portions toward the outside of the dish (see photo, below). Sprinkle and pat on any remaining coating. Micro-cook, covered loosely with paper towels, on high for 12 to 14 minutes or till chicken is no longer pink, rearranging the pieces after half the cooking time. Makes 4 servings.

Arranging the chicken pieces with the meatiest portions toward the outside of the dish helps ensure even cooking in the microwave oven.

Five Spice Sesame Chicken

Total time: 30 minutes

12	sesame toast crackers, crushed (½ cup)
1	tablespoon sesame seed
½	teaspoon five spice powder
¼	teaspoon salt
¼	teaspoon paprika

● For coating, in a shallow dish combine crushed crackers, sesame seed, five spice powder, salt, and paprika.

2	to 2½ pounds meaty chicken pieces (breasts, wings, thighs, and drumsticks)
2	tablespoons milk

● On waxed paper brush each chicken piece with milk. Roll pieces in coating mixture to coat on *3* sides.

In a 12x7½x2-inch nonmetal baking dish arrange chicken pieces on a nonmetal rack with *uncoated* side down and the meatiest portions toward the outside (see photo, below left). Micro-cook, loosely covered with paper towels, on 100% power (high) for 12 to 14 minutes or till chicken is no longer pink, rearranging the pieces after half the cooking time. Makes 4 servings.

Because five spice powder is basically a blend of five household spices, it's a cinch to make your own if you have a few minutes to spare. Just combine 1 teaspoon ground *cinnamon*, 1 teaspoon crushed *aniseed*, ¼ teaspoon crushed *fennel seed*, ¼ teaspoon ground *pepper*, and ⅛ teaspoon ground *cloves*. Store in a tightly covered container. Or, if you prefer, look for five spice powder in the Oriental foods section of your grocery store.

Attention Microwave Owners

Microwave recipes were tested in countertop microwave ovens that operate on 600 to 700 watts. Cooking times are approximate since microwave ovens vary by manufacturer. If yours has fewer watts, foods may take a little longer to cook.

Spinach Tomatoes

Total time: 40 minutes

1	**10-ounce package frozen chopped spinach**
¾	**pound ground raw turkey**

● In a 1-quart casserole cook spinach, covered, on 100% power (high) for 7 minutes, stirring once. Drain and squeeze out excess water. Set spinach aside.

In the same dish crumble ground turkey. Cook, covered, for 3 to 5 minutes or till meat is no longer pink, stirring once. Drain.

4	**large tomatoes (about 2 pounds)**
1	**beaten egg**
¼	**cup fine dry Italian-seasoned crumbs**
¼	**cup grated Parmesan cheese**
¼	**teaspoon onion powder**
¼	**teaspoon dried oregano, crushed**

● Meanwhile, cut a ¼-inch slice off the tops of the tomatoes. Scoop out the tomato pulp, leaving a ¼-inch shell. Invert on paper towels to drain.

In a medium mixing bowl stir together egg, bread crumbs, Parmesan cheese, onion powder, oregano, and ¼ teaspoon *pepper.* Stir in turkey and spinach.

Salt and pepper
Parmesan cheese

● Sprinkle insides of tomato shells with salt and pepper. Fill *each* with ¼ of the turkey mixture. Top with additional Parmesan cheese. Place in an 8x8x2-inch baking dish. Cook, uncovered, on high for 4 to 6 minutes or till heated through, giving dish a half-turn once. Serves 4.

Cranberry-Raisin-Sauced Chicken

Total time: 15 minutes

2 **whole large skinned and boned chicken breasts, halved lengthwise**	● Place chicken pieces in a 10x6x2-inch nonmetal baking dish. Micro-cook, covered with vented, microwave-safe plastic wrap, on 100% power (high) for 8 to 10 minutes or till no longer pink, turning pieces over and rearranging once. Drain. Keep chicken warm.
1 **8-ounce can whole cranberry sauce** ¼ **cup raisins** 1 **tablespoon brown sugar** **Dash ground cloves**	● In a 2-cup glass measure combine cranberry sauce, raisins, brown sugar, and cloves. Micro-cook, uncovered, on high for 1 to 2 minutes or till heated through, stirring once. Pour sauce over chicken to serve. Makes 4 servings.

You'll be the quickest draw in the kitchen when you serve up this saucy chicken dish. Tart cranberries teamed with sweet raisins and a dash of spice will soon have it on your family's "most wanted" list.

Coriander Chicken

Total time: 20 minutes

1 **tablespoon butter *or* margarine** 1 **teaspoon lemon juice** 1 **teaspoon ground coriander** ¼ **teaspoon onion powder** ⅛ **teaspoon chili powder**	● In an 8x8x2-inch or 10x6x2-inch nonmetal baking dish combine butter or margarine, lemon juice, coriander, onion powder, and chili powder. Micro-cook, uncovered, on 100% power (high) for 45 seconds or till butter or margarine is melted. Stir to mix well.
1 **whole large skinned and boned chicken breast, halved lengthwise**	● Dip chicken breast halves in butter mixture to coat well. Arrange in the dish. Cook, covered loosely with waxed paper, on high for 4 to 6 minutes or till chicken is no longer pink, turning pieces over and rearranging once.
1½ **teaspoons all-purpose flour** 1 **teaspoon brown sugar** **Dash ground red pepper** ¼ **cup chicken broth (see tip, page 19)** **Lemon slices (optional)** 1 **cup cooked vegetables (optional)**	● Transfer chicken to a serving platter, reserving liquid. Keep chicken warm. For sauce, in a 2-cup glass measure combine flour, brown sugar, and red pepper. Stir in reserved liquid till smooth. Add chicken broth. Cook, covered, on high for 1 to 2 minutes or till the mixture is thickened and bubbly, stirring every 30 seconds. Cook for 30 seconds more. Serve the sauce over chicken and cooked vegetables, if desired. Garnish with lemon slices, if desired. Serves 2.

Ground coriander is made from the seeds of the Chinese parsley or cilantro plant. The flavor will remind you of a combination of lemon and sage—completely compatible with poultry.

Photo-Finish Turkey Loaf

Total time: 35 minutes

1 beaten egg
1 cup soft bread
  crumbs (1½ slices)
½ cup alfalfa sprouts,
  snipped
1 small green pepper, finely
  chopped (⅓ cup)
1 tablespoon dried minced
  onion
¼ teaspoon ground ginger
¼ teaspoon salt
¼ teaspoon pepper
1 pound ground raw turkey

● In a medium mixing bowl stir together the egg, bread crumbs, alfalfa sprouts, green pepper, onion, ginger, salt, and pepper. Add ground turkey. Mix well.

In a 9-inch nonmetal pie plate shape the ground turkey mixture into a ring, 6 inches in diameter, with a 2-inch hole in the center.

You'll be first under the wire when this high-performance meat loaf is your entry in the race to beat the mealtime clock.

Sweet-and-sour
  barbecue sauce

● Micro-cook, covered loosely with waxed paper, on 100% power (high) for 7 to 9 minutes or till turkey is no longer pink, giving dish a quarter-turn every 3 minutes. Drizzle meat with *about ¼ cup* of the barbecue sauce. Let stand for 5 minutes. Transfer to a serving plate. Pass additional barbecue sauce. Serves 4.

Turkey Cassoulet

Total time: 20 minutes

½ pound ground raw turkey
1 medium onion, chopped
  (½ cup)
¼ teaspoon garlic powder

● In a 1½-quart nonmetal casserole crumble ground turkey. Add onion and garlic powder. Micro-cook, covered, on 100% power (high) for 3 to 5 minutes or till turkey is no longer pink, stirring once to break up meat. Drain.

The composition of a true French cassoulet is unknown because ingredients vary from region to region, but you'll find our turkey version continues in the best tradition of this hearty stew.

½ pound smoked turkey
  sausage, cut into
  ½-inch pieces
1 15-ounce can great
  northern beans
1 8-ounce can tomato sauce
½ teaspoon instant beef
  bouillon granules
¾ teaspoon dried thyme,
  crushed
¼ teaspoon pepper
1 bay leaf

● Stir in sausage pieces, *undrained* beans, tomato sauce, bouillon granules, thyme, pepper, and bay leaf. Cook, covered, on high for 6 to 8 minutes or till heated through, stirring twice. Remove bay leaf. Makes 4 servings.

Photo-Finish Turkey Loaf

Turkey Enchiladas

Total time: 35 minutes

½ **pound ground raw turkey**
1 **cup mild salsa**
½ **cup sliced pitted ripe olives**
⅛ **teaspoon garlic powder**

● In a 1-quart nonmetal casserole crumble ground turkey. Micro-cook, covered, on 100% power (high) for 3 to 4 minutes or till no longer pink, stirring once. Drain. Stir in the salsa, olives, and garlic powder.

Our Test Kitchen Home Economists recommend using the thickest salsa available to help keep the tortillas crisp.

1 **8-ounce container soft-style cream cheese with chives and onion**
6 **6-inch flour tortillas**
1 **cup shredded Monterey Jack cheese *or* cheddar cheese (4 ounces)**

● Spread about *2 tablespoons* of the cream cheese with chives on *each* tortilla. Spoon about ⅓ *cup* of the turkey mixture down the center of *each* torilla. Roll up tortillas and place, seam side down, in a greased 10x6x2-inch nonmetal baking dish. Cook, covered with vented plastic wrap, on high for 4 to 6 minutes or till heated through, giving dish a half-turn once. Top tortillas with the shredded cheese. Cook, uncovered, for 1 to 1½ minutes more or till cheese is melted. Serves 4 to 6.

Quick Chicken Saltimbocca

Total time: 30 minutes

1 **whole large skinned and boned chicken breast, halved lengthwise**

● Place each chicken breast half, boned side up, between 2 pieces of clear plastic wrap. Working from the center to the edges, pound the chicken lightly with the fine-toothed or flat side of a meat mallet, forming a rectangle about ⅛ inch thick (see photo, page 26). Remove the wrap.

1 **2.5-ounce package very thinly sliced turkey ham**
1 **slice Swiss cheese, halved**
½ **of a small tomato, peeled, seeded, and chopped**
1 **tablespoon butter *or* margarine**
2 **tablespoons fine dry seasoned bread crumbs**
 Paprika

● For *each* chicken roll, place *half* of the turkey ham on a chicken breast half, folding ham, if necessary, to fit. Place *1* half-slice of Swiss cheese on the ham, near one edge. Top with *half* of the tomato. Fold in sides of chicken and roll up jelly-roll style, starting from edge with cheese (see photo, right).
In a shallow nonmetal baking dish micro-cook the butter on 100% power (high) for about 20 seconds or till melted. Place chicken rolls, seam side down in the shallow baking dish. Roll chicken in the melted butter coat. Sprinkle with bread crumbs and paprika.

Fold the sides of the chicken piece toward the center and then roll it up jelly-roll style.

 Tomato slices (optional)
 Fresh parsley (optional)

● Micro-cook, uncovered, on 70% power (medium-high) for 5 to 7 minutes or till chicken is no longer pink, giving dish a half-turn *every* 2 minutes. Garnish with sliced tomato and parsley sprigs, if desired. Makes 2 servings.

Plum-Good Chicken

Total time: 30 minutes

⅓ cup plum preserves
2 teaspoons soy sauce
2 to 2½ pounds meaty
   chicken pieces (breasts,
   wings, thighs, and
   drumsticks), skinned
   if desired

● In a small bowl stir together plum preserves and soy sauce. Brush chicken pieces on all sides with plum mixture. Arrange chicken pieces in a 12x7½x2-inch nonmetal baking dish with the meatiest portions of the chicken toward the outside of dish (see photo, page 38).
   Cook, covered loosely with waxed paper, on 100% power (high) for 12 to 14 minutes or till chicken is no longer pink, rearranging pieces and basting with juices after half the cooking time. Remove chicken from dish, reserving juices. Keep warm.

Don't be surprised to see a rich brown-colored sauce instead of a plum-colored sauce. The soy sauce may disguise the color of the plum preserves, but it certainly enhances the flavor.

¼ cup orange juice
1 tablespoon cornstarch
   Hot cooked rice (optional)

● Pour the reserved juices into a 2-cup glass measure. Skim fat from juices, if necessary. Combine the orange juice and cornstarch. Stir into reserved juices. Micro-cook, uncovered, on high for 2 to 3 minutes or till mixture is thickened and bubbly, stirring every 30 seconds. Micro-cook for 30 seconds more. Serve over chicken pieces with hot cooked rice, if desired. Makes 4 servings.

Mostaccioli Turkey

Total time: 40 minutes

1½ cups mostaccioli
     (4 ounces)
  1 pound turkey breakfast
     sausage
  1 small onion, chopped
  1 small carrot, shredded
  1 7½-ounce can tomatoes,
     cut up
  1 6-ounce can Italian-style
     tomato paste
  ⅔ cup water
  ⅛ teaspoon garlic powder

● Cook mostaccioli according to package directions. Rinse and drain in a colander. Set aside.
   Meanwhile, in a 2-quart nonmetal casserole, crumble turkey sausage. Add onion and carrot. Micro-cook, covered, on 100% power (high) for 5 to 7 minutes or till turkey sausage is no longer pink and vegetables are crisp-tender, stirring twice to break up meat. Drain if necessary. Stir in *undrained* tomatoes, tomato paste, water, garlic powder, and cooked mostaccioli.

Cooking pasta in your microwave oven takes about the same time as cooking it conventionally, so we suggest cooking the mostaccioli on your range top. That way, you can prepare the meat and sauce in the microwave and have them ready to layer as soon as the pasta is done.

1 beaten egg
1 cup ricotta cheese *or*
   cream-style cottage
   cheese, drained
¼ cup grated Parmesan
   cheese
½ teaspoon dried oregano,
   crushed

● For the cheese mixture, in a small mixing bowl stir together the egg, ricotta cheese or cottage cheese, Parmesan cheese, and oregano.
   Place *half* of the turkey mixture in a 10x6x2-inch nonmetal baking dish. Spread the cheese mixture atop. Top with remaining meat mixture. Cook, covered, on high for 10 to 12 minutes or till heated through, giving dish a half-turn every 3 minutes. Makes 4 servings.

Honey of a Chicken

Total time: 35 minutes

½ teaspoon finely shredded
    orange peel
½ cup orange juice
2 tablespoons honey
1 tablespoon soy sauce
2 teaspoons cornstarch

● For sauce, in a 2-cup glass measure, stir together orange peel, orange juice, honey, soy sauce, and cornstarch. Micro-cook on 100% power (high) for 2 to 3 minutes or till mixture is thickened and bubbly, stirring every minute. Set aside.

2 to 2½ pounds meaty
    chicken pieces (breasts,
    wings, thighs, and
    drumsticks)

● In a 12x7½x2-inch nonmetal baking dish arrange chicken pieces, skin side down, with meatiest portions facing toward the outside (see photo, page 38). Cook, covered loosely with waxed paper, on high for 9 minutes, giving dish a half-turn and rearranging chicken once. Drain well. Brush chicken with sauce. Turn chicken and brush with sauce again. Cook, covered, for 8 to 10 minutes or till chicken is no longer pink. Remove baking dish from oven. Keep warm. Reheat remaining sauce, uncovered, for 1 minute or till heated through. Pass with chicken. Serves 4.

Micro-Plus Grilled Chicken: Prepare as above, *except* after cooking chicken for 9 minutes, transfer to a preheated grill. Arrange chicken, skin side down, directly over *medium* coals. Brush with sauce and grill for 10 minutes. Turn and brush with sauce. Grill for 8 to 10 minutes more or till chicken is done, brushing several times with sauce.

Sour Cream Turkey Burgers

Total time: 35 minutes

1 **8-ounce carton sour cream dip with bacon and horseradish _or_ with blue cheese**	● In a large mixing bowl stir together _half_ of the sour cream dip, the bread crumbs, green onions, salt, and pepper. Add ground turkey. Mix well. Shape mixture into four ¾-inch-thick patties.	**Kiss the burger blahs bye-bye! Horseradish adds a mildly piquant taste that enhances ground turkey for a truly better burger.**
½ **cup fine dry bread crumbs**		
4 **green onions, sliced**		
¼ **teaspoon salt**		
⅛ **teaspoon pepper**		
1 **pound ground raw turkey**		
2 **tablespoons cooking oil**	● In a 10-inch skillet cook patties in hot oil over medium-high heat for 6 to 8 minutes or till patties are no longer pink, turning once.	
4 **hamburger buns, split and toasted**	● Serve patties on buns, topped with some of the remaining sour cream dip, a tomato slice, and a lettuce leaf. Serves 4.	
4 **tomato slices**		
4 **lettuce leaves**		
	Broiling directions: Prepare burgers as above, _except_ place patties on an unheated rack in a broiler pan. Broil 3 to 4 inches from the heat for 5 minutes. Turn patties and broil for 4 to 6 minutes more or till done.	

Garlic Linguine

Total time: 35 minutes

6 ounces linguine, green
   linguine, *or* spaghetti
2 whole medium skinned
   and boned chicken
   breasts
1 small onion, chopped
4 cloves garlic, minced
½ teaspoon dried basil,
   crushed
2 tablespoons butter *or*
   margarine

● Cook linguine or spaghetti according to package directions. Drain well.
   Meanwhile, cut chicken into 1½-inch pieces. In a 12-inch skillet cook onion, garlic, and basil in butter or margarine over medium-high heat for 2 minutes, stirring occasionally. Add chicken and stir-fry for 3 minutes.

Garlic lovers, unite! It is possible to enjoy this pungent herb in polite society if you build in the cure for "Dragon breath" as the garnish. Trim each plate with a sprig of fresh parsley. Then chew on it after dinner and no one will ever know you indulged.

2 small zucchini, sliced
   ¼ inch thick
1 cup sliced fresh
   mushrooms
1 medium tomato, chopped
¼ teaspoon salt
¼ teaspoon pepper

● Add zucchini and mushrooms. Reduce the heat. Cook, covered, over medium-low heat for 5 to 6 minutes or till chicken is no longer pink and zucchini is crisp-tender. Uncover and cook for 1 to 2 minutes more or till liquid has evaporated. Stir in linguine or spaghetti, tomato, salt, and pepper. Heat through. Makes 4 servings.

Apple-Pecan Chicken

Total time: 30 minutes

1 cup pecan halves	● Preheat the oven to 350°. Place pecans in a shallow baking dish. Bake for 8 to 10 minutes or till toasted.
2 whole large skinned and boned chicken breasts, halved lengthwise **⅓ cup cranberry *or* cranberry-apple juice cocktail** **1 tablespoon brown sugar** **1½ teaspoons cornstarch** **⅛ teaspoon ground nutmeg** **⅛ teaspoon ground cinnamon**	● Meanwhile, cut chicken into 1-inch pieces. For sauce, in a small mixing bowl stir together cranberry or cranberry-apple juice cocktail, brown sugar, cornstarch, nutmeg, and cinnamon. Set aside.
1 tablespoon cooking oil **⅔ cup cranberries**	● Preheat a wok or large skillet over high heat. Add cooking oil. Add *half* of the chicken to wok or skillet. Stir-fry for 2 to 3 minutes or till no longer pink. Remove chicken. Repeat with remaining chicken. Return all chicken to wok or skillet. Stir in cranberries. Push mixture to sides.
1 large green apple, sliced	● Stir sauce. Add to center of wok or skillet. Cook and stir till thickened and bubbly. Cook and stir for 30 seconds more. Stir in apple slices. Cook, covered, for 2 minutes. Stir in the toasted pecan halves. Serve immediately. Serves 4.

Pecans are genuine, wholesome, made-in-America originals. Early colonists were introduced to the native nut by the Indians, and it has become an important part of our cuisine.

Total time: 25 minutes

Walnut-Orange Chicken

⅔ cup long grain rice
2 whole large skinned and
  boned chicken breasts
½ cup orange juice
2 tablespoons soy sauce
1 tablespoon dry sherry
1½ teaspoons cornstarch
1 teaspoon grated fresh
  gingerroot
½ cup chopped walnuts

● Cook rice according to package directions. Meanwhile, cut the chicken into 1-inch pieces. For sauce, in a small mixing bowl stir together the orange juice, soy sauce, dry sherry, cornstarch, and gingerroot. Set mixture aside.

In a 10-inch skillet cook walnuts over medium heat till toasted, stirring frequently. Remove nuts.

2 tablespoons cooking oil
2 green onions, thinly sliced
1 orange, peeled, separated
  into segments, and cut
  into pieces

● Add cooking oil to the hot skillet. Stir-fry onions for 30 seconds. Add *half* of the chicken. Stir-fry for 2 to 3 minutes or till chicken is no longer pink. Remove chicken and onions. Stir-fry remaining chicken for 2 to 3 minutes or till done. Return chicken and onions to skillet.

Stir sauce and add to skillet. Cook and stir till mixture is thickened and bubbly. Cook for 1 to 2 minutes more. Stir in walnuts and orange segments. Serve over rice. Makes 4 servings.

Fresh orange segments, toasted walnuts, and a hint of gingerroot blended with chicken are a flavor sensation certain to be a hit at your house.

Total time: 20 minutes

Jarlsberg Turkey

¼ cup all-purpose flour
½ teaspoon lemon pepper *or*
  pepper
⅓ cup fine dry bread crumbs
⅓ cup finely shredded
  Jarlsberg *or* Swiss
  cheese (1½ ounces)
4 turkey breast slices
  (about 8 ounces)
1 beaten egg

● In a plastic bag combine the flour and lemon pepper or pepper. In a shallow dish stir together the bread crumbs and shredded cheese.

One at a time, add turkey slices to flour mixture and shake to coat. Dip turkey slices into the egg and then into the cheese mixture, coating evenly.

3 tablespoons butter *or*
  margarine
1 lemon, cut into wedges

● In a large skillet melt butter or margarine. Cook turkey slices over medium heat about 4 minutes or till turkey is lightly browned on both sides and no longer pink, turning once. Serve with lemon wedges. Makes 4 servings.

Wonderful for cooking, Jarlsberg cheese is a Swiss-like cheese from Norway, with a nutty, slightly buttery flavor. It's the headline in this crispy coating for turkey breast slices.

Gingered Chicken Pitas

Total time: 40 minutes

1	**whole large skinned and boned chicken breast**
2	**tablespoons dry sherry**
2	**tablespoons soy sauce**
2	**teaspoons cornstarch**
1	**teaspoon grated fresh gingerroot** *or* **¼ teaspoon ground ginger**
	Dash bottled hot pepper sauce

● Cut chicken into thin bite-size strips. For sauce, in a small bowl stir together the dry sherry, soy sauce, cornstarch, gingerroot or ground ginger, hot pepper sauce, and 2 tablespoons cold *water*. Set mixture aside.

1	**tablespoon cooking oil**
½	**of a small head cabbage, coarsely chopped (3 cups)**
3	**green onions, sliced**

● Preheat a wok or large skillet over medium-high heat. Add cooking oil (add more oil as necessary during cooking). Stir-fry cabbage and onions in hot oil for 3 minutes. Remove vegetables from wok or skillet.

2	**large pita bread rounds, halved**

● Add chicken to wok or skillet. Stir-fry for 3 minutes or till chicken is no longer pink. Push chicken from the center of wok or skillet. Stir sauce. Add to center of the wok or skillet. Cook and stir till thickened and bubbly. Cook and stir for 30 seconds more.

Return vegetables to wok or skillet. Cook and stir for 1 minute more. Spoon mixture into pita bread halves. Serve immediately. Makes 2 servings.

It's hard to beat the aroma of fresh gingerroot. Keeping some on hand is no problem either. For short-term storage, wrap the root in paper towels and refrigerate. For longer storage, gingerroot keeps nicely up to three months in the refrigerator in a closed container, if you cover the peeled slices with dry sherry. Or, freeze the unpeeled gingerroot and cut off what you need while it's still frozen.

Cheesy Chicken Chowder

Total time: 25 minutes

1 **10-ounce package frozen mixed vegetables** 1¾ **cups chicken broth (see tip, page 19)** 1 **medium onion, chopped** 1 **teaspoon prepared mustard** ¼ **teaspoon pepper**	● In a large saucepan stir together frozen vegetables, chicken broth, onion, mustard, and pepper. Bring to boiling.
⅓ **cup corkscrew macaroni *or* other small pasta**	● Stir in macaroni. Reduce the heat. Simmer, covered, for 7 to 10 minutes or till pasta is tender, stirring occasionally.
1¾ **cups milk** 1 **cup cubed cooked chicken** 2 **tablespoons all-purpose flour**	● Stir in *1½ cups* of the milk and chicken. Stir remaining milk into flour till smooth. Stir into chicken mixture. Cook and stir till mixture is thickened and bubbly. Cook and stir for 1 minute more.
1 **cup shredded process Swiss *or* sharp American cheese**	● Add cheese. Cook and stir till cheese is melted. Makes 4 servings.

Few things warm the stomach or the soul as well as chicken noodle soup. Try our cheesy version. It's a creamy twist to a generation-jumping favorite.

Italian Turkey Sausage Soup

Total time: 45 minutes

½ small head cabbage, shredded (4 cups)
1 medium onion, chopped
2 tablespoons olive *or* cooking oil

● In a Dutch oven cook cabbage and onion in olive or cooking oil till vegetables are crisp-tender.

A close cousin of classic Italian minestrone, this hearty main-dish soup has an added attraction: smoked turkey sausage.

3½ cups chicken broth (see tip, page 19)
1 16-ounce can tomatoes, cut up
1 15-ounce can great northern beans
12 ounces smoked turkey sausage link, cut into ¼-inch slices
1 cup loose-pack frozen peas
¼ cup small pasta
1 teaspoon Italian seasoning
¼ teaspoon garlic powder
Dash pepper
Parmesan cheese (optional)

● Stir in chicken broth, *undrained* tomatoes, *undrained* beans, sliced turkey sausage, peas, pasta, Italian seasoning, garlic powder, and pepper. Bring to boiling. Reduce the heat. Cook, covered, over medium-low heat for 10 to 15 minutes or till pasta is tender. Sprinkle each serving with Parmesan cheese, if desired. Makes 6 servings.

Microwave reheating directions: To reheat 1 serving of soup, micro-cook it in a microwave-safe container, loosely covered with waxed paper, on 100% power (high) for 3 to 5 minutes or till heated through, stirring once.

Corn and Lima Chowder

Total time: 25 minutes

2 slices bacon, cut in half
1½ cups water
1 medium potato, peeled and chopped
1 9- or 10-ounce package frozen corn and lima beans (succotash)
1 tablespoon instant chicken bouillon granules
½ teaspoon dried dillweed
⅛ teaspoon pepper

● In a large saucepan cook bacon till crisp. Drain and crumble. Set aside.
  In the same saucepan combine water, potato, corn and lima beans, bouillon granules, dillweed, and pepper. Bring to boiling. Reduce the heat. Simmer, covered, for 10 to 12 minutes or till vegetables are crisp-tender.

"Merci beaucoup" to the French peasants who first developed soup as we know and love it today. However, give some credit to the royalty. If Louis XIV of France hadn't decided soup was food fit for the aristocracy, its fame never would have spread so far.

1½ cups milk
3 tablespoons all-purpose flour
1½ cups cubed cooked chicken *or* turkey
3 green onions, sliced (¼ cup)

● Stir *1 cup* of the milk into saucepan. Stir remaining milk into flour. Stir flour mixture into saucepan. Cook and stir till thickened and bubbly. Cook and stir for 1 minute more. Stir in chicken or turkey and green onions. Heat through. Top each serving with some of the crumbled bacon. Makes 4 servings.

Microwave reheating directions: To reheat 1 serving of soup, micro-cook it in a microwave-safe container, loosely covered with waxed paper, on 100% power (high) for 3 to 5 minutes or till heated through, stirring once.

Curried Chowder

Total time: 35 minutes

1 medium apple, cored and chopped (1¼ cups)
2 stalks celery, sliced (1 cup)
1 to 1½ teaspoons curry powder
3 tablespoons butter *or* margarine
3 tablespoons all-purpose flour
1⅔ cups chicken broth (see tip, page 19)
1½ cups milk

● In a medium saucepan cook the apple, celery, and curry powder in butter or margarine for 4 to 5 minutes or till apple and celery are crisp-tender. Stir in flour. Add chicken broth and milk all at once. Cook and stir over medium heat till mixture is thickened and bubbly.

Cooking the curry powder in butter helps take the edge off the spice, leaving only a deliciously well-rounded flavor.

1½ cups cubed cooked chicken
½ cup raisins
¼ chopped peanuts

● Stir in chicken and raisins. Cook and stir over medium heat for 5 minutes or till heated through, stirring occasionally. Top each serving with some of the chopped peanuts. Makes 4 servings.

Keg o' Chili

Keg o' Chili

Total time: 30 minutes

1 pound ground raw turkey
1 medium onion, chopped
2 15-ounce cans chili beans
  in chili gravy
1 12-ounce can beer
1 7½-ounce can tomatoes,
  cut up
½ cup chili sauce
1 teaspoon chili powder
¼ teaspoon garlic salt
¼ teaspoon crushed red
  pepper

● In a large saucepan or Dutch oven cook and stir ground turkey and onion till turkey is no longer pink and onion is tender. Stir in *undrained* beans, beer, *undrained* tomatoes, chili sauce, chili powder, garlic salt, and red pepper.

You'll be a dine-o-mite success when you serve up this chili at your next tailgate party or family dinner. But if feeding a small army isn't for you, freeze the chili in 2-cup (1-serving) portions and use it as ammunition the next time you're caught off guard at mealtime.

Shredded cheddar cheese
  (optional)
Chopped green pepper
  (optional)

● Bring to boiling. Reduce the heat. Cook over medium-low heat for 15 to 20 minutes or till heated through, stirring occasionally. Top each serving with cheese and green pepper, if desired. Makes 4 or 5 servings.

Mumbo Gumbo

Total time: 30 minutes

¾ cup long grain rice
1 12-ounce can spicy
  vegetable juice cocktail
1 12-ounce can whole
  kernel corn with sweet
  peppers
1 10-ounce package frozen
  cut okra
1 7½-ounce can tomatoes,
  cut up
1 tablespoon dried minced
  onion
1 teaspoon instant chicken
  bouillon granules
1 teaspoon Worcestershire
  sauce
½ teaspoon dried thyme,
  crushed
¼ teaspoon garlic powder
¼ teaspoon bottled hot
  pepper sauce

● Cook rice according to package directions. Meanwhile, in a large saucepan stir together the vegetable juice cocktail, *undrained* corn, okra, *undrained* tomatoes, onion, bouillon granules, Worcestershire sauce, thyme, garlic powder, and hot pepper sauce. Cook, covered, over medium-low heat for 10 to 12 minutes or till okra is crisp-tender, stirring occasionally.

Although traditional gumbos are thickened with filé powder, we've used the thickening power of okra to save you time.

2½ cups cubed cooked
  chicken

● Stir in chicken. Cook for 5 to 7 minutes more or till heated through. Serve over the hot cooked rice. Makes 4 or 5 servings.

Chicken-Vegetable Platter

Total time: 30 minutes

2 eggs

● Place eggs in a small saucepan. Add *warm* water to cover. Bring to boiling over high heat. Reduce the heat. Simmer, covered, for 15 minutes. Pour off hot water. Fill saucepan with ice water. Let stand for 5 minutes. Peel and quarter eggs.

Sesame-Herb Dressing
1½ **cups cubed cooked chicken**
 2 **cups cauliflower flowerets *and/or* thinly sliced cucumber**
 1 **small tomato, cut into wedges**
 1 **small carrot, thinly sliced**

● Meanwhile, prepare Sesame-Herb Dressing. Place chicken in a small bowl. Pour dressing over chicken. Chill in the refrigerator for 15 minutes. Transfer chicken to a serving platter with a slotted spoon, reserving dressing.

Arrange the chicken, vegetables, and eggs in groups on the serving platter. Pass reserved dressing. Makes 4 servings.

If you have a little extra time, arrange individual salads on lettuce-lined plates for a bit more personal touch.

Sesame-Herb Dressing: In a screw-top jar combine ¼ cup *cooking oil;* 3 tablespoons dry white *wine* or *vinegar;* 2 tablespoons *lemon juice;* 1 tablespoon *sugar;* 1 teaspoon dried *basil,* crushed; ½ teaspoon *salt;* ½ teaspoon *sesame seed;* ¼ teaspoon dried *rosemary,* crushed; and several dashes bottled *hot pepper sauce.* Stir in ½ to 1 teaspoon *sesame oil,* if desired. Cover and shake well.

Turkey Briefs

Become acquainted with the many new turkey products available. Most are convenient, quick, and versatile, as you'll be able to tell by looking at the recipes in this book. To help you recognize them, here is a quick rundown of the most common ones.

Turkey steaks
Cut from a prime whole muscle on the inside of the breast, turkey steaks weigh between 4 and 8 ounces each.

Turkey sausage
Made of ground turkey, *smoked* turkey sausage is cured, spiced, and smoked to give traditional flavor.

Ground turkey
Ground turkey can be a mixture of white and dark meat or all dark meat. It's available frozen in 1-pound tubes or packaged fresh, in varying weights.

Turkey breast portions
Available roasted, smoked, barbecued or unseasoned, these boneless, fully-cooked, and ready-to-eat white meat portions are found in varying weights in the fresh meat case.

Breast slices (cutlets)
Skinless and boneless white meat slices from the breast are about ¼ inch thick and weigh about 2 ounces each.

Turkey ham
Turkey ham (and pastrami) is skinless and boneless thigh meat, smoked and cured to taste similar to traditional ham (and pastrami).

Sesame Chicken Salad

Total time: 30 minutes

3 tablespoons sesame seeds
1 6-ounce package frozen
  pea pods

● In a medium skillet cook sesame seeds over medium heat about 5 minutes or till toasted, stirring occasionally.
  Meanwhile, place pea pods in a colander. Run colander under cool water till thawed. Drain well.

---

1 8-ounce can pineapple
  chunks
½ of a small head lettuce,
  shredded, *or* 4 cups
  torn mixed greens
2 cups cubed cooked
  chicken
1 stalk celery, chopped
½ of an 8-ounce can sliced
  water chestnuts, drained

● Drain pineapple chunks, reserving *1 tablespoon* of the juice. Set aside.
  In a large bowl combine the pineapple chunks, lettuce or mixed greens, chicken, celery, water chestnuts, pea pods, and sesame seeds. Toss to mix well.

¼ cup cooking oil
1 tablespoon honey
1 tablespoon soy sauce
2 teaspoons coarse-grain
  brown mustard
½ teaspoon sesame oil

● In a screw-top jar combine the reserved pineapple juice, cooking oil, honey, soy sauce, mustard, and sesame oil. Shake well. Pour over chicken mixture. Toss to coat well. Serves 4.

Try a chicken salad that brings the aura of the Far East to your table. It's versatile and refreshing, not just another salad.

The Mango Tango Salad

Total time: 30 minutes

1 15-ounce can mango
  slices
1 2½-ounce package sliced
  almonds
2 cups cubed cooked
  chicken *or* turkey
1½ cups seedless red grapes

● Place the can of mangoes in the freezer. If desired, toast almonds by placing them in a single layer in a shallow baking pan. Bake in a 350° oven about 10 minutes or till toasted, stirring occasionally. In a large mixing bowl toss together chicken or turkey, grapes, and almonds. Set aside.

¼ cup lemon yogurt
¼ cup mayonnaise *or* salad
  dressing
¾ teaspoon dried dillweed
⅛ teaspoon salt
⅛ teaspoon pepper
  Lettuce leaves
1 kiwi fruit, peeled and
  sliced (optional)

● In a small mixing bowl stir together yogurt, mayonnaise or salad dressing, dillweed, salt, and pepper. Fold into the chicken mixture. Drain and halve mango slices. Gently fold into the chicken mixture. Serve the salad on lettuce leaves. Garnish with kiwi fruit, if desired. Makes 4 servings.

Substitute fresh mango when it's in season from May to August. Look for mangoes that are smooth and firm, then let them ripen at room temperature till they soften. The juicy fruit reminds many people of a cross between pineapple and apricot.

Chicken-Garbanzo Toss

Total time: 35 minutes

1 15-ounce can garbanzo
  beans, drained
1½ cups cubed cooked
  chicken
2 stalks celery, sliced
1 small green pepper,
  seeded and chopped
2 green onions, sliced
  (optional)

½ cup mayonnaise *or* salad
  dressing
2 tablespoons lemon juice
¼ teaspoon chili powder
⅛ teaspoon onion powder
6 ounces shredded
  Monterey Jack cheese
  with jalapeño peppers
  (1½ cups)
Lettuce leaves
1 tomato, cut into wedges
1 avocado, seeded, peeled,
  and sliced (optional)

● In a medium mixing bowl combine garbanzo beans, chicken, celery, green pepper, and green onions, if desired.

● For dressing, in a small bowl combine mayonnaise, lemon juice, chili powder, onion powder, ¼ teaspoon *salt*, and ⅛ teaspoon *pepper*. Stir dressing into bean mixture. Stir in *half* of the shredded cheese. Chill in freezer about 15 minutes. Serve on lettuce leaves garnished with remaining cheese, tomato wedges, and avocado slices, if desired. Serves 4.

Just when you think there can't possibly be a new chicken salad, along comes our upscale green-pepper-and-garbanzo version. It's sure nice to be surprised every once in a while.

Total time: 25 minutes

Cool Cuke Turkey Salad

½ cup dairy sour cream *or* plain yogurt
2 tablespoons mayonnaise or salad dressing
1 tablespoon milk (optional)
2 teaspoons dried dillweed *or* 2 tablespoons snipped fresh dillweed
1 green onion, sliced
¼ teaspoon pepper

● For dressing, in a small mixing bowl stir together sour cream or yogurt; mayonnaise or salad dressing; milk, if desired; dillweed; green onion; and pepper. Set aside.

Surprise guests? No worries. Keep your cool and in 20 minutes you can be sitting down to eat this refreshing salad. Simply marvelous!

8 ounces smoked turkey breast portion, cut into ½-inch cubes
1 small cucumber, halved and thinly sliced
½ cup cashews *or* walnuts
Lettuce leaves *or* alfalfa sprouts

● In a medium mixing bowl combine turkey, cucumber, and cashews or walnuts. Pour dressing over all and toss to coat. Serve on lettuce leaves or alfalfa sprouts. Makes 3 servings.

Pita Pizza Salads

Total time: 30 minutes

1 10-ounce package frozen chopped spinach
2 large pita bread rounds

● Cook spinach according to package directions. Drain, squeezing out excess liquid. Separate pita rounds into circles by slitting pitas around the outside and gently pulling apart the halves.

Pick this peck of pita pizzas, cause if you pick *these* pita pizzas, you'll have picked a pizza and a pretty salad, too!

½ of an 8-ounce container soft-style cream cheese with chives and onion
1 medium tomato, seeded and chopped (¾ cup)
¼ cup sliced pitted ripe olives
8 slices turkey ham, chopped

● Preheat the broiler. In a medium mixing bowl combine spinach, cream cheese, tomato, and olives. Toss to coat mixture well.
  Lay ¼ of the chopped turkey atop *each* pita circle. Broil 3 inches from the heat for 1 minute. Spread *each* pita circle with ¼ of the spinach mixture. Return to broiler for 1 minute.

1 cup shredded Swiss cheese (4 ounces)

● Sprinkle ¼ of the cheese atop *each* pita circle. Broil about 2 minutes or till cheese starts to melt. Serves 4.

Bulgur Chicken Salad

Total time: 40 minutes

¾ cup bulgur 1½ cups boiling water	● Place bulgur in a bowl. Pour boiling water over bulgur. Let stand for 20 minutes. Drain well.
⅓ cup olive *or* salad oil ⅓ cup lemon juice 1 teaspoon dried mint, crushed ½ teaspoon lemon pepper ¼ teaspoon garlic salt	● Meanwhile, for dressing, in a screw-top jar combine the olive or salad oil, lemon juice, mint, lemon pepper, and garlic salt. Shake to mix well.
2 cups cubed cooked chicken 2 medium tomatoes, peeled, seeded, and chopped 1 small cucumber, seeded and chopped ¾ cup snipped parsley	● In a large mixing bowl combine the drained bulgur, chicken, tomato, cucumber, and parsley. Toss to mix well.
½ cup chopped pecans Lettuce leaves	● Shake dressing well. Pour over chicken mixture. Toss gently to coat. Place chicken mixture in freezer for 10 minutes to chill. (Keeps up to 2 days in the refrigerator.) Stir in pecans just before serving. Serve the salad on lettuce leaves. Makes 4 servings.

It's not a mirage! By softening the bulgur in boiling water, we've eliminated the need to marinate this traditional Middle Eastern salad overnight. Now you can relish it right away.

German Pastrami Salad

Total time: 30 minutes

1 pound new potatoes,
   quartered
1 cup loose-pack frozen
   cut green beans

● In a medium saucepan cook potatoes and green beans, covered, in a small amount of boiling water about 15 minutes or just till tender. Drain well.

---

1 8-ounce package turkey
   pastrami, cut into bite-
   size strips
1 8-ounce can kidney beans,
   drained
1 small onion, chopped
3 tablespoons olive *or*
   cooking oil
3 tablespoons red wine
   vinegar
1 teaspoon dry mustard
½ teaspoon dried dillweed
¼ teaspoon sugar
⅛ teaspoon salt
⅛ teaspoon pepper
   Lettuce *or* spinach leaves

● Meanwhile, in a large bowl combine turkey pastrami, kidney beans, and onion. Add the potatoes and beans.
   For dressing, in a screw-top jar combine olive or cooking oil, vinegar, mustard, dillweed, sugar, salt, and pepper. Shake well. Pour dressing over turkey mixture. Toss to coat well. Serve the salad on lettuce or spinach leaves. Makes 4 servings.

Not all salads are cold side dishes. Here's a hot, whole-meal salad patterned after German-style potato salad. The turkey pastrami spices up the mixture and adds protein.

Greek Chicken Salad

Total time: 30 minutes

1 cup loose-pack frozen
   green beans
2 cups cubed cooked
   chicken
1 medium cucumber,
   seeded and chopped
1 cup crumbled feta cheese
1 cup sliced fresh
   mushrooms
½ cup sliced pitted ripe
   olives

● In a medium saucepan cook green beans in a small amount of boiling water for 5 to 6 minutes or till beans are crisp-tender. Drain. Rinse with cold water. Let stand covered with cold water.
   Meanwhile, in a large mixing bowl combine chicken, cucumber, feta cheese, mushrooms, and olives. Set salad in the freezer while preparing the dressing.

Insomnia, bad breath, dandruff, wrinkles, and thinning hair—yogurt cures them all, or so it was once believed. Although yogurt can't really do it all, it *can* provide foods with a light, tangy taste, and you with a good source of many vitamins and minerals.

½ cup mayonnaise *or* salad
   dressing
¼ cup plain yogurt
¼ teaspoon garlic powder
¼ teaspoon pepper
   Lettuce leaves

● For dressing, in a small mixing bowl combine mayonnaise or salad dressing, yogurt, garlic powder, and pepper.
   Drain green beans and add to chicken mixture. Pour dressing over chicken mixture. Toss to coat. Serve on lettuce leaves. Makes 4 servings.

Dressed-Up BLTs

Total time: 35 minutes

8 slices bacon
2 whole large skinned and
   boned chicken breasts,
   halved lengthwise

● In a 10-inch skillet cook bacon over medium heat till crisp. Drain, reserving *2 tablespoons* of the drippings in the skillet. Set bacon aside.

Meanwhile, place *each* chicken breast half, boned side up, between 2 pieces of clear plastic wrap. Working from the center to the edges, pound the chicken lightly with the fine-toothed or flat side of a meat mallet to ¼-inch thickness (see photo, page 26).

● Cook chicken pieces in reserved bacon drippings over medium heat for 2 to 3 minutes or till lightly browned. Turn and cook for 2 to 3 minutes more or till chicken is no longer pink.

¼ cup mayonnaise *or* salad
   dressing
1 tablespoon catsup
½ teaspoon Worcestershire
   sauce
¼ teaspoon prepared
   horseradish
4 individual French rolls,
   split and toasted
1 medium tomato, thinly
   sliced
   Lettuce leaves

● Meanwhile, in a small mixing bowl stir together mayonnaise or salad dressing, catsup, Worcestershire sauce, and horseradish. Spread roll halves with some of the mayonnaise mixture.

For sandwiches, top each roll bottom with lettuce and a piece of chicken. Layer with *2* pieces of bacon, some of the tomato, and more lettuce. Top with the roll top, spread side down. Serves 4.

Dare to deck out your next sandwich in style. Here we've dressed up a BLT with a sautéed chicken breast fillet and a zippy sauce. Presented on a toasted French roll, it's definitely a chic-wich!

Total time: 25 minutes

Garden Delight Sandwich

2 eggs	● Place eggs in a small saucepan. Add warm water to cover. Bring to boiling over high heat. Reduce the heat. Simmer, covered, for 15 minutes. Pour off hot water. Fill saucepan with *cold* water. Let stand for 2 minutes. Peel and slice the eggs.
⅓ cup mayonnaise *or* salad dressing 2 to 3 teaspoons prepared horseradish 1 teaspoon dried dillweed 6 radishes, chopped (⅓ cup)	● Meanwhile, in a small bowl stir together mayonnaise or salad dressing, horseradish, and dillweed. Stir in chopped radishes.
4 slices pumpernickel bread 4 ounces very thinly sliced chicken *or* turkey ½ small cucumber, thinly sliced	● For *each* sandwich, spread *half* of the mayonnaise mixture on *2* bread slices. Layer spread side of *1* slice with *half* of the chicken or turkey, egg, and cucumber slices. Top with the remaining bread slice, spread side down. Serves 2.

Chill the hard-cooked eggs more quickly by placing ice cubes in the cold water.

Total time: 30 minutes

Pineapple-Cheese Rolls

½ of an 8-ounce container soft-style cream cheese with pineapple 2 tablespoons milk 1 cup cubed cooked chicken *or* turkey, *or* one 5½-ounce can chunk-style chicken, drained and broken up 1 4-ounce package shredded cheddar cheese (1 cup) 1 small carrot, shredded ¼ cup toasted pecans *or* almonds, chopped (optional) Dash ground nutmeg	● In a medium mixing bowl stir together cream cheese and milk. Stir in chicken or turkey; cheddar cheese; carrot; nuts, if desired; and nutmeg. Place in the freezer for 10 to 15 minutes to chill.
3 kaiser rolls 3 lettuce leaves	● Cut rolls in half horizontally. For *each* sandwich, spread ⅓ of the chicken mixture on the roll bottom. Top with a lettuce leaf and roll top. Serves 3.

Because this sandwich filling is chock-full of goodies, it is fairly stiff. We suggest you serve it on kaiser rolls or a firm-textured bread.

Total time: 20 minutes

Turkey-Veggie Pitas

Pictured on pages 4-5.

¼ cup mayonnaise *or* salad dressing	● For dressing, in a small mixing bowl stir together mayonnaise or salad dressing, chutney, curry, and pepper.
2 tablespoons chutney	
¼ to ½ teaspoon curry powder	
⅛ teaspoon pepper	

Sandwiches are a natural stage for demonstrating the versatility of turkey. Here it's starring with avocado, cheese, tomato, sprouts, and chutney-curry dressing, presented in a pita bread half.

1 small avocado, seeded, peeled, and sliced	● Toss avocado slices with lemon juice to prevent browning. For *each* sandwich spread inside of pita half with some of the dressing. Place *1* cheese slice in each pita half. Add ¼ of the turkey slices, tomato slices, and alfalfa sprouts. Top with ¼ of the avocado slices and some of the remaining dressing. Serve immediately. Makes 4 servings.
1 tablespoon lemon juice	
2 large pita bread rounds, halved	
4 thin slices provolone *or* Swiss cheese (4 ounces)	
5 ounces thinly sliced smoked turkey breast portion	
1 medium tomato, sliced	
1 cup fresh alfalfa sprouts	

You'll find that two 2½-ounce packages of very thinly sliced turkey or chicken make a great understudy for the sliced turkey breast portion.

Total time: 25 minutes

Zucchini-Chicken Salad Sandwiches

2 5-ounce cans chunk-style chicken	● Drain chicken. Cut up large pieces. In a mixing bowl combine mayonnaise or salad dressing, mustard, onion powder, and pepper. Mix well. Stir in chicken, zucchini, and celery.
¼ cup mayonnaise *or* salad dressing	
1 tablespoon horseradish mustard	
¼ teaspoon onion powder	
⅛ teaspoon pepper	
¾ cup shredded zucchini	
¼ cup sliced celery	

Now here's an original way to use up that extra zucchini that always seems to find its way into refrigerators. The horseradish mustard gives this splendid spin-off of the routine chicken salad sandwich just the gusto it needs.

8 slices rye *or* whole wheat bread	● Toast bread, if desired. For *each* sandwich, place ¼ of the chicken mixture on *1* slice of bread. Top a with lettuce leaf and another slice of bread. Makes 4 servings.
4 lettuce leaves	

Chinese Chicken-Fried Rice

Total time: 45 minutes

1 11-ounce package frozen herb-buttered rice	● Place rice pouch in a pan of hot water. Let stand for 10 to 15 minutes or till almost thawed.
2 whole medium skinned and boned chicken breasts **⅓ cup dry sherry** **2 tablespoons soy sauce** **1 teaspoon cornstarch** **¼ teaspoon garlic powder**	● Meanwhile, cut chicken into bite-size strips. In a small mixing bowl stir together sherry, soy sauce, cornstarch, and garlic powder. Set aside.
Nonstick spray coating **2 beaten eggs**	● Spray wok or large skillet with non-stick spray coating. Pour in beaten eggs. Cook, covered, over medium-high heat about 2 minutes or till eggs are set in the center and lightly browned around the edges. Carefully loosen and invert onto a cutting board. Cut eggs into 2x1½-inch pieces. Set aside.
1 tablespoon cooking oil **1½ cups loose-pack frozen Oriental vegetables**	● Add cooking oil to wok or skillet. Add vegetables. Stir-fry for 3 to 4 minutes or till crisp-tender. Remove vegetables. Add *half* of the chicken and stir-fry for 2 to 3 minutes or till no longer pink, adding more oil if necessary. Remove chicken. Repeat with remaining chicken.
1 tablespoon cooking oil	● Add cooking oil to wok or skillet. Add rice to wok or skillet, tossing constantly for 3 to 4 minutes or till golden brown. Stir in soy mixture. Cook and stir till thickened and bubbly. Stir in vegetables and chicken. Add egg strips and heat through. Makes 4 servings.

Total time: 25 minutes

Chicken Véronique

2 tablespoons butter *or*
   margarine
2 whole large skinned and
   boned chicken breasts,
   halved lengthwise

● In a 10-inch skillet melt butter or margarine. Cook chicken in butter over medium-high heat about 10 minutes or till meat is no longer pink, turning once. Remove chicken from skillet, reserving juice. Keep chicken warm.

⅓ cup chicken broth
   (see tip, page 19)
1½ teaspoons cornstarch
1 tablespoon orange
   marmalade
½ teaspoon lemon juice
¼ cup whipping cream
½ cup seedless green *or*
   red grapes, halved

● For sauce, stir chicken broth into cornstarch. Add to reserved juice in skillet. Stir in orange marmalade and lemon juice. Cook and stir over medium heat till mixture is thickened and bubbly. Cook and stir for 1 minute more. Stir in cream. Add grapes and cook for 2 to 3 minutes or till heated through, stirring often. Serve sauce over chicken pieces. Makes 4 servings.

The traditional French "Véronique" refers to a dish garnished with seedless green grapes. Our taste panel so liked the color that seedless red grapes added, we decided they should be an option as well.

Total time: 35 minutes

Chicken-Cabbage Chow Mein

2 whole large skinned and
   boned chicken breasts,
   halved lengthwise
1 cup chicken broth
   (see tip, page 19)
2 tablespoons oyster sauce
   or 1 tablespoon soy
   sauce
4 teaspoons cornstarch

● Cut chicken into thin bite-size strips. Set aside. In a bowl stir chicken broth and oyster sauce or soy sauce into cornstarch. Set aside.

2 tablespoons cooking oil
2 teaspoons grated fresh
   gingerroot
6 green onions, bias-sliced
   into 1-inch pieces
1 carrot, thinly bias sliced
1 cup shredded cabbage
1 3-ounce can chow mein
   noodles

● In a wok or 10-inch skillet, heat cooking oil. Stir-fry gingerroot in hot oil over high heat for 30 seconds. Add green onions and carrot. Stir-fry for 3 minutes. Remove from wok. (Add more oil, if necessary.) Stir-fry *half* of the chicken for 2 to 3 minutes or till no longer pink. Remove from wok. Repeat with remaining chicken. Return all chicken to the wok and push to sides. Stir chicken broth mixture and stir into wok. Cook and stir till mixture is thickened and bubbly. Return vegetables to wok. Add cabbage. Cook, covered, for 1 minute or till heated through. Serve over chow mein noodles. Serves 4.

Oyster sauce is a kitchen staple of Oriental cooks. Made of oysters cooked in soy sauce and brine, it's lighter in color and thicker than soy sauce, but every bit as salty. It adds a subtle and unique flavor, but in a pinch soy sauce works equally well.

Microwave Manicotti

Total time: 40 minutes

4 manicotti shells
1 tablespoon cooking oil
1 beaten egg
½ cup ricotta *or* cream-
    style cottage cheese,
    drained
½ cup shredded mozzarella
    cheese (2 ounces)
2 tablespoons grated
    Parmesan cheese

● In a 1½-quart nonmetal casserole combine manicotti shells, oil, and 3 cups *hottest tap water*. Micro-cook, uncovered, on 100% power (high) for 12 to 14 minutes or till almost done, rearranging shells twice. Cover dish and set aside.

Meanwhile, in a small bowl combine the egg, ricotta or cottage cheese, mozzarella cheese, Parmesan cheese, and ¼ teaspoon *pepper*. Set aside.

The trick to manicotti in 40 minutes is making the most of your microwave. In this recipe, cooking the manicotti in just 3 cups of water saves you the time of boiling a big pot of water on the range top.

½ pound ground raw turkey
1 cup meatless spaghetti
    sauce with mushrooms
½ teaspoon dried minced
    onion
¼ teaspoon Italian
    seasoning, crushed
    Snipped parsley (optional)

● In a 1-quart nonmetal casserole crumble ground turkey. Micro-cook covered, on high for 2 to 3 minutes or till turkey is no longer pink, stirring twice. Drain. Stir in spaghetti sauce, onion, and Italian seasoning. Drain manicotti shells and rinse under cold water.

Using a spoon, stuff ¼ of the cheese mixture into *each* shell. Pour *half* the meat mixture into a 10x6x2-inch baking dish. Place stuffed shells atop. Top with remaining sauce, completely covering shells. Cook, covered with vented plastic wrap, on high for 4 to 5 minutes or till heated through, giving dish a half-turn once. Garnish with parsley, if desired. Serves 2.

Spicy Chicken Fajitas

Total time: 30 minutes

8 8-inch flour tortillas	● Preheat the oven to 350°. Wrap stack of tortillas in foil. Heat in the oven for 15 minutes to soften.

2 whole large skinned and boned chicken breasts, halved lengthwise
1 6-ounce can hot-style vegetable juice cocktail
1 tablespoon cornstarch
½ teaspoon instant chicken bouillon granules
¼ teaspoon garlic powder
¼ to ½ teaspoon ground red pepper
1 medium avocado, seeded, peeled, and chopped
1 teaspoon lemon juice
	● Meanwhile, cut chicken into thin bite-size strips.
	  For sauce, in a small bowl stir together the vegetable juice cocktail, cornstarch, bouillon granules, garlic powder, and ground red pepper. Set aside.
	  Toss together avocado and lemon juice to coat. Set aside.

1 small zucchini 1 tablespoon cooking oil 3 green onions, cut into 1-inch bias slices	● Cut zucchini in half crosswise. Cut each half into lengthwise strips. Preheat a large skillet or wok over high heat. Add cooking oil (add more oil as necessary during cooking). Stir-fry zucchini and onions over high heat for 2 to 3 minutes or till the vegetables are crisp-tender. Remove vegetables from skillet or wok.
	● Add *half* of the chicken to skillet or wok. Stir-fry for 2 to 3 minutes or till chicken is no longer pink. Remove chicken. Stir-fry remaining chicken for 2 to 3 minutes or till done. Return all chicken to skillet or wok. Push chicken to sides.
⅓ cup salsa	● Stir sauce, then add to center of skillet or wok. Cook and stir till thickened and bubbly. Cook and stir for 1 minute more. Return vegetables to skillet. Add salsa. Stir to coat with sauce. Cook, covered, for 1 minute or till heated through.
Dairy sour cream 1 4-ounce package shredded cheddar cheese (1 cup)	● To serve, at the table let each person pile some of the chicken and vegetable mixture, avocado, sour cream, and cheese onto the warm tortillas. Roll or fold into bundles. Makes 4 servings.

Say hello to chicken with a Tex-Mex accent. Although traditional fajitas are made from marinated beef skirt steak, chicken versions are rapidly catching on.

Total time: 25 minutes

Mediterranean Turkey Burgers

1 beaten egg
½ cup soft bread crumbs
¼ cup chopped, pitted ripe olives
1 tablespoon dried parsley flakes
¼ teaspoon garlic powder
¼ teaspoon ground cinnamon
⅛ teaspoon ground nutmeg
1 pound ground raw turkey

● Preheat the broiler. In a mixing bowl stir together egg, bread crumbs, olives, parsley, garlic powder, cinnamon, and nutmeg. Add ground turkey. Mix well.

Shape meat mixture into four ½-inch-thick patties. Place patties on an unheated rack in a broiler pan. Broil 3 to 4 inches from the heat for 5 minutes. Turn patties and broil for 4 to 6 minutes more or till no longer pink.

To eat or not to eat a burger? You won't have to ponder that question once you've caught a whiff of this classically Greek-flavored burger. It's true mealtime inspiration.

½ of a medium cucumber, very thinly sliced
4 hamburger buns, split
4 tomato slices
Plain yogurt *or* dairy sour cream
¼ cup crumbled feta cheese

● For *each* burger, place ¼ of the cucumber slices on the bottom half of a bun. Top with a meat patty, tomato slice, some of the yogurt or sour cream, ¼ of the feta cheese, and bun top. Serves 4.

Grilling directions: Prepare as above, *except* grill patties on an uncovered grill directly over *medium* coals for 5 minutes. Turn patties and grill for 4 to 5 minutes more or till done.

Szechwan Chicken

Total time: 40 minutes

¾ cup long grain rice
2 whole large skinned and boned chicken breasts, halved lengthwise

● Cook rice according to package directions. Meanwhile, cut chicken into thin bite-size strips.

2 tablespoons dry sherry
1 to 2 tablespoons hot bean sauce
1 tablespoon soy sauce
¾ teaspoon Szechwan peppercorns, crushed
½ teaspoon sesame oil
⅛ teaspoon ground red pepper

● In a small mixing bowl stir together the dry sherry, hot bean paste, soy sauce, peppercorns, sesame oil, and red pepper. Set mixture aside.

2 tablespoons cooking oil
2 medium carrots, bias sliced
½ head bok choy *or* Chinese cabbage, chopped
1 medium green pepper, seeded and coarsely chopped (2 to 3 cups)
3 green onions, bias sliced

● Preheat a wok or large skillet. Add cooking oil. Stir-fry carrots for 2 minutes. Add bok choy or chinese cabbage, green pepper, and onions. Stir-fry for 2 minutes more or till vegetables are crisp-tender. Remove vegetables from wok or skillet.

● Add more oil, if necessary. Add half of the chicken to the wok or skillet. Stir-fry for 2 to 3 minutes or till chicken is no longer pink. Remove chicken. Stir-fry remaining chicken for 2 to 3 minutes or till done. Return all chicken to wok or skillet. Push chicken to sides.

● Stir soy sauce mixture into wok or skillet. Stir in vegetables to coat. Cook, uncovered, for 1 minute or till heated through. Serve with rice. Serves 4.

This dish isn't for the faint of heart. Szechwan, a western province of China, is known for its hot 'n' spicy dishes. With our version, however, you can regulate the temperature of this fiery food by the amount of hot bean sauce you add.

Index

Have BETTER HOMES AND
GARDENS® magazine delivered to
your door. For more information,
write to: MR. ROBERT AUSTIN
P.O. BOX 4536
DES MOINES, IA 50336.